THE DADA MARKET

An Anthology of Poetry

Translated and with
an Introduction
by Willard Bohn

Southern Illinois University Press
Carbondale and Edwardsville

Frontispiece photograph courtesy of Anita Bohn.

Library of Congress Cataloging-in-Publication Data

The Dada market : an anthology of poetry / translated and
with an introduction by Willard Bohn.
        p.   cm.
    Poems by forty-two poets writing in seven languages.
    Includes bibliographical references.
    1. Poetry, Modern—20th century—Translations into
    English.   2. Dadaism.   I. Bohn, Willard, 1939–
PN6101.D3   1993
808.81'04—dc20   91-45283
ISBN 0-8093-1818-0 (cloth) — ISBN 0-8093-1819-9 (pbk.) CIP

The paper used in this publication meets the minimum
requirements of American National Standard for Information
Sciences—Permanence of Paper for Printed Library Materials,
ANSI Z39.48-1984. ⊚

For my daughter Heather —
may you remain young forever.

Il est difficile à tout le monde, même à un
prêtre, de vivre sans un dada.

—Balzac, *Le Curé de Tours*

Contents

Illustrations

Acknowledgments

Grateful acknowledgment is made to the following for permission to include poems for which they hold the copyright.

To The Francis Bacon Foundation, Claremont, California, for Walter Conrad Arensberg: "Ing," "Arithmetical Progression of the Verb 'To Be,'" and "Theorem."

To Editions Pierre Belfond for Francis Picabia: "Tambourin," "L'Oeil froid," "L'Enfant," "Tous les jours," "Bonheur," and "Fleur coupée." From *Ecrits 1913–1920*, edited by Oliver Revault d'Allonnes. Copyright 1975 by Editions Pierre Belfond, Paris.

To DuMont Buchverlag for Kurt Schwitters: "Gedicht No. 48," "Es ist Herbst," and "An Anna Blume." From *Das literarische Werk*, edited by Friedhelm Lach. Copyright 1973–1981 by DuMont Buchverlag, Cologne.

To Editions Gallimard for Pierre Albert-Birot: "Rasoir mécanique," an excerpt from *La Joie des sept couleurs*, and "Catastrophe." From *Poésie 1916–1924*. Copyright © 1967 by Editions Gallimard, Paris. For André Breton: "Pièce fausse." From *Oeuvres complètes*, edited by Marguerite Bonnet et al. Copyright © 1988 by Editions Gallimard, Paris. For Paul Eluard: "Max Ernst" and "La Grande Maison inhabitable." From *Oeuvres complètes*, edited by Marcelle Dumas and Lucien Scheler. Copyright © 1968 by Editions Gallimard, Paris.

To Editions Gérard Lebovici for Georges Ribemont-Dessaignes: "Trombone à coulisse" and "Elle a les seins . . ." From *Dada: manifestes, poèmes, articles, projets, 1915–1930*, edited by Jean-Pierre Begot. Copyright 1974 by Editions Gérard Lebovici, Paris.

To Arche Verlag for Richard Huelsenbeck: "Flüsse." From *Phantastische Gebete*. Copyright © 1960 by Verlag A. G. Die Arche, Zurich. For Ferdinand Hardekopf: "Splendeurs et misères des débrouillards." From *Hans Arp/Richard Huelsenbeck/Tristan Tzara: DADA Gedichte*. Copyright © 1957 by Verlag A. G. Die Arche, Zurich.

x   Acknowledgments

To Limes Verlag for Hans (Jean) Arp: "Bim Bim ausglim . . ." From *Der Pyramidenrock*. Copyright © by Limes Verlag, Munich, and Hans Arp.

To Anabas-Verlag for Johannes Baader: "Fifi." From *Johannes Baader-Oberdada: Schriften, Manifeste, Flugblätter, Billets, Werke und Taten*, edited by Hanne Bergius et al. Copyright 1977 by Anabas-Verlag, Giessen. For Raoul Hausmann: "bbbb . . ." and "kp'erioum." From *Das Lachen DADAs* by Hanne Bergius. Copyright 1989 by Anabas-Verlag, Giessen. And from *Am Anfang war Dada*, edited by Karl Riha and Günter Kämpf. Copyright 1972 and 1991 by Anabas-Verlag, Giessen.

To Editions Flammarion for Tristan Tzara: "Le Marin," "La Panka," "Sage Danse deux," and "Printemps." From *Oeuvres complètes*, edited by Henri Béhar. Copyright 1975–1977 by Editions Flammarion, Paris.

To Roger L. Conover, Mina Loy's literary executor, for excerpts from "Love Songs."

To Limes Verlag for Hans (Jean) Arp: "Weh unser guter Kaspar ist tot," in: Hans Arp, *Gesammelte Gedichte*, Volume I. Copyright © by Limes Verlag in F. A. Herbig Verlagsbuchhandlung, Munich.

To Robert Cowley for Malcolm Cowley: "Towards a More Passionate Apprehension of Life."

To Ré Soupault for Philippe Soupault: "Salutations distinguées," "Flamme," and "Les Sentiments sont gratuits."

Last but not least I would like to thank Carol Burns, of Southern Illinois University Press, for invaluable editorial assistance in preparing the manuscript for publication. This volume has benefited not only from her fine eye for detail but from her advice on numerous occasions.

Introduction: Shopping for Dada

Dada is an artichoke.

—Francis Picabia, "Dada philosophique"

Dada fills tubes of paint with margarine.

—Georges Ribemont-Dessaignes, "Les Plaisirs de Dada"

Although the word *Dada* first appeared in Zurich in 1916, the origins of the movement itself were more diffuse. Invented by Tristan Tzara on 8 February 1916, if we are to believe Hans (Jean) Arp's farcical account, the name described a phenomenon that was by no means limited to Switzerland.[1] In the first place, the Dada spirit already existed in several other countries where it had emerged as an extreme form of avant-garde activity. Thus, as Arp himself proclaimed, "There were Dadaists before the name Dada existed for Dada, before the Dadaists were Dada."[2] Viewed in this perspective, terms such as *pre-Dada* and *proto-Dada* become totally meaningless when applied to these earlier manifestations. In attempting to delimit a historical period, these terms confuse chronological considerations with aesthetics. In the second place, Dada quickly became an international movement and spread throughout the European continent. By 1920 Walter Conrad Arensberg could write, "Dada is American, Dada is Russian, Dada is Spanish, Dada is Swiss, Dada is German, Dada is French, Belgian, Norwegian, Swedish, Monacan."[3] He might have added that it was also Italian, Hungarian, Yugosla-

---

1. Hans (Jean) Arp, "Déclaration," *Dada au Grand Air*, Sept. 1921, 4.
2. Cited in José Pierre, *Le Futurisme et le dadaïsme* (Lausanne: Rencontre, 1967), 69.
3. Walter Conrad Arensberg, "Dada est américain," *Littérature* 13 (May 1920): 15.

vian, Dutch, Czechoslovakian, Polish, and Romanian. "In those days,"
Marcel Janco later recalled, "Dada was in the air everywhere."[4]
José Pierre has provided what is probably the most accurate de-
scription to date of the movement's origins. "If the term was invented in
Zurich," he writes, "the Dada spirit first became evident in New
York. . . . Baptized in Switzerland in 1916, the infant (conceived in Paris)
was actually born in New York in 1915."[5] As he observes, the embryonic
experience in Paris was crucial for the development of Dada. Although
relatively brief (1912–14), this period saw the emergence of two central
figures, Marcel Duchamp and Francis Picabia, and a host of other impor-
tant personalities. In addition to the events usually cited during this pe-
riod, Picabia, Guillaume Apollinaire, Marius de Zayas, and Alberto
Savinio collaborated on a Dada pantomime that they intended to per-
form in New York.[6] The recent discovery of this work indicates that the
presence of the Dada spirit in Paris was more intense than previously
recognized. After the outbreak of the World War I, Duchamp and Pica-
bia settled in New York where they proved to be important catalysts.
Their arrival followed the appearance of the first Dada review by several
months. Entitled *291*, the review was published by a group of American
Dadaists centered around Alfred Stieglitz and his review *Camera Work*.[7]
Another contingent of equal importance met at Arensberg's apartment at
33 West 67th Street. Together the two groups welcomed the French art-
ists, who were soon joined by friends and family, and with their aid suc-
ceeded in creating the first true Dada movement anywhere.

As noted, 1916 marked the appearance of Zurich Dada, which
arose independently, and the publication of the review *Cabaret Voltaire*.
Named after the artistic cabaret founded by Hugo Ball, it was broadly
eclectic and gave way to *Dada* in 1917. The nominal leader of the group,
Ball was soon eclipsed by the flamboyant Tzara who provided de facto
leadership. The group itself consisted of Romanian expatriates and for-

    4. Cited in Manuel L. Grossman, *Dada: Paradox, Mystification, and
Ambiguity in European Literature* (New York: Bobbs-Merrill, 1971), 48.
    5. Pierre, *Le Futurisme et le dadaïsme*, 69.
    6. See Willard Bohn, *Apollinaire and the Faceless Man: The Creation
and Evolution of a Modern Motif* (Rutherford, N.J.: Fairleigh Dickinson
University Press, 1991).
    7. For a study of these and other little reviews in America during
this period, see Dickran Tashjian, *Skyscraper Primitives: Dada and the
American Avant-Garde, 1910–1925* (Middletown, Conn.: Wesleyan Univer-
sity Press, 1975).

mer German Expressionists. While they were highly accomplished poets and artists, like their colleagues elsewhere, their real specialty was theatrical performance. A third Dada faction was situated in Barcelona during the war. Revolving about an art gallery owned by Josep Dalmau, it included numerous French expatriates in addition to Catalan artists and writers such as Joan Miró and Josep Maria Junoy. Arising independently in 1916, the Barcelona branch picked up momentum with Picabia's arrival in 1917. The first four issues of *391*, which he founded during his stay, provided an additional focus for Dada activity and set the tone for the remainder of the period.

   With the end of World War I, a radical realignment of Dada forces occurred. Although the original three groups continued, the balance of power swung from countries situated on the war's periphery to two of the principal antagonists: Germany and France. Beginning in 1919, the German branch consisted of three different factions. Dominated by Richard Huelsenbeck and Raoul Hausmann, Berlin Dada was motivated above all by political concerns. In addition to satirizing politics in their art, its members sought to foment social revolution. Centered around Arp and Max Ernst on the one hand and around Kurt Schwitters on the other, Cologne Dada and Hanover Dada were somewhat less political. Although the three groups dissolved a few years later, while they existed they were a potent force for social and artistic change. Only Schwitters continued to pursue his Dada activities, in Hanover, until the Nazis drove him out fifteen years later. In postwar Paris, the movement coalesced about four young men who were later to found Surrealism: André Breton, Philippe Soupault, Louis Aragon, and Paul Eluard. Before long they were joined by Picabia and Duchamp, who participated joyously in the general uproar, and by several other major figures. These included Man Ray, who arrived from New York, Arp, Ernst, and Tzara himself. By the end of 1923, however, Dada had ceased to exist as an (un)organized movement in France or anywhere else. Although some members, such as Picabia and Schwitters, remained faithful to the Dada spirit all their lives, most became Surrealists or developed other interests.

   Dada's geographical distribution and diversity have caused one recent critic to speak of "the Dada movements" as opposed to a single unified school.[8] Despite its diversity, however, the movement as a whole

   8. Charles Russell, *Poets, Prophets, and Revolutionaries: The Literary Avant-Garde from Rimbaud through Postmodernism* (New York: Oxford University Press, 1985), 97–121.

was surprisingly cohesive. This is all the more astonishing when one recalls that there was no central committee, no governing body of any kind, to impose unity or to determine the direction Dada should take. Interestingly, when Breton tried to organize such a committee in 1922, it spelled the death of Paris Dada. Writing to Guillermo de Torre from Zurich in 1919, Tzara suggested that, paradoxically, the movement's lack of direction was responsible for its essential unity. "Dada is constantly changing and evolving," he wrote, "in order to maintain a certain continuity between tendencies that are not regulated. Rather than a coordinated, finalist movement, it is a joyful way of life."[9] This statement provides valuable insight into the Dada endeavor and the paradoxical mechanism governing it. Among other things, it reiterates the Dadaists' frequent claim that Dada was a philosophy of life rather than an artistic credo. Given the movement's fierce opposition to any form of authority, moreover, there was no way that a rigid framework could be imposed on its members or their activities.

This anarchic spirit is perhaps best exemplified by the list of seventy-five "presidents" of Dada, published in the *Bulletin Dada* on 5 February 1920. Not only were all true Dadaists against Dada, as a slogan proclaimed in the same issue, but each and every member was president of the movement. In view of its antiauthoritarian stance, as Tzara makes clear, Dada adopted a self-regulating mechanism based on an organic model. Rather than constrain existing activities to fit a preexisting model, which would have necessitated creating a hierarchy of aesthetic and ethical values, Dada chose to accommodate itself to these activities. Rejecting the role of censorship for that of liberation, it continued to grow and to redefine itself as it evolved. More than anything, this organic dynamism provided continuity among members and among the movement's successive phases. Additional cohesion was furnished by an "interlocking directorship" of sorts that participated in the various Dada activities (especially the reviews). Not only were the different groups in constant contact with one another, but they collaborated on each other's projects to an unprecedented degree.

Historically speaking, the critical response to Dada has been grossly inadequate since the movement's inception. Although Surrealism has managed to garner a certain amount of respectability, Dada was widely regarded as anathema until fairly recently. For many years Robert

9. Quoted in Guillermo de Torre, "Kaleidoscopio," *Ultra* 1,3 (20 Feb. 1921): 4.

Motherwell's anthology *The Dada Painters and Poets*, originally published
in 1951, was the only work in English to take the movement seriously.
John Henderson's remarks about avant-garde experimentation provide a
useful framework in which to view this problem. "The proper function
of the avant-garde," he observes, "to widen the frontiers of the possible
both in form and content by the process of experiment, will generally
elicit a hostile reaction from the orthodox. . . . The danger is that the
avant-gardist will be tempted merely to shock received opinion in order
simply to *provoke* such reaction, which is not necessarily the same
thing."[10] Since Dada venerated all forms of scandalous behavior, the
largely negative reaction is not difficult to understand. Like most of the
readers and viewers who were exposed to Dada shock and provocation,
critics have assumed that the movement was a hoax. Even today many
observers continue to view Dada as a purely destructive phenomenon
whose only virtue was that it paved the way for Surrealism. Various re-
marks by the original participants have only confirmed them in their
opinion. Thus, Aragon once commented, "I have never sought anything
else but scandal, and I have sought it for itself." And Tzara was fond of
proclaiming, "There is a great negative work of destruction to be accom-
plished."

Another reason for Dada's neglect is that its works have seemed to
be impervious to critical analysis. For one thing, they embody a current
of irrationalism that was intensified by the outbreak of the war and by
the resultant breakdown of social values. For another, their aesthetic
strategies depend on the deliberate misuse of convention. Utilizing the
techniques of subversion, distortion, and disruption, Dada compositions
are fanatically antilogical.[11] In the Dada rebellion against bourgeois val-
ues in life and in art, logic was considered a correlative of traditional au-
thority, both of which were condemned for corrupting and imprisoning
humankind. Faced with irrational texts of bewildering complexity, the
poor critics could only throw up their hands in despair. Helmut Hatz-
feld, for example, in an important book published in 1952, was forced to
conclude that Dada was a kind of infantile behavior. "The literary critic is
helpless before the waking-dream infantilism of a Dadaist like Robert
Desnos," he confessed, "when he says, 'Dans le sommeil de Rose Sélavy

10. John A. Henderson, *The First Avant-Garde 1887–1894: Sources of
the Modern French Theatre* (London: Harrap, 1971), 52.
11. J. H. Matthews discusses these techniques as dramatic princi-
ples in *Theatre in Dada and Surrealism* (Syracuse, N.Y.: Syracuse Univer-
sity Press, 1974); see especially p. 274.

il y a un nain sorti d'un puits qui vient manger son pain la nuit.'"[12] For-
tunately, the situation is no longer quite so desperate. The last twenty
years have seen an increasing interest in Dada and a series of landmark
studies by authors such as Mary Ann Caws, J. H. Matthews, Michel San-
ouillet, and Henri Béhar. There are even two journals, *Dada/Surrealism*
and *Le Siècle Eclaté*, that are devoted to this subject. If the movement is
still somewhat resistant to analysis, it has nevertheless yielded many of
its secrets and is no longer forbidding. As an example, Desnos' utterance
is no longer very mysterious ("In the sleep of Rose Sélavy, there is a
dwarf who has emerged from a well who comes to eat her bread at night").
The French version is simply an example of a *contrepet* (spoonerism), a
mechanical procedure for generating everything from images to myths.

One critic attributes the reemergence of Dada into contemporary
consciousness to the similarity between the present age and the original
era.[13] This thesis is certainly tempting, as is the parallel he draws be-
tween two periods overwhelmed by war and technology. Even more tell-
ing is the appearance of the neo-Dada and Pop movements—the latest in
an impressive series of Dada derivatives including the Theater of the Ab-
surd and Abstract Expressionism. With the rediscovery of Dada in a
sympathetic social context, the positive side of the movement has finally
come to light. For if Dada displayed numerous destructive tendencies, its
constructive aspects were at least as important. Most critics attribute the
presence of these two contradictory elements to the duality of destruc-
tion and construction inherent in the creative act itself, exacerbated in
the case of Dada by the war. Discussing the avant-garde mechanism in
general, Charles Russell gives a perfect description of Dada dynamics:

> At the heart of avant-garde aesthetic activity is the dynamic ten-
> sion between the poles of negation and creation, between the as-
> sault on the given world and its aesthetic tradition and the search
> for the basis of a new culture and its art. . . . However, since the
> future is unknown and often unimaginable, the nihilistic impulse
> in the avant-garde artwork is often the most dramatic expression of
> avant-garde desire. . . . In effect, the avant-garde frequently "ad-
> vances" more by pushing away from the known than by identify-
> ing a distinct goal toward which it moves.[14]

12. Helmut A. Hatzfeld, *Literature Through Art: A New Approach to
French Literature* (1952; reprint, Chapel Hill: University of North Carolina
Press, 1969), 202.
13. Grossman, *Dada*, xiii.
14. Russell, *Poets, Prophets, and Revolutionaries*, 34.

The Dadaists in particular wanted to wipe the slate clean so that they would be free to create whatever they felt like. Having reduced artistic expression to its bare essentials—sound and typography in poetry; sound, gesture, and action in theater; color and line in art—they began to experiment with new, uncorrupted forms. Besides reconstructing reality to conform more closely to contemporary experience, they adopted an antiart stance that revolutionized art and literature. Many years later Picasso stated: "Paintings are but research and experiment. I never do a painting as a work of art."[15] If this attitude no longer surprises us, it is because Dada has helped establish the concept of art as a dynamic, constantly evolving entity.

Dada's one overriding concern was the achievement of total liberty: social, moral, and intellectual. In this vein, its adherents questioned the basic postulates of rationalism and humanism as few had done before. Taking as their watchword Tzara's declaration "Thought is made in your mouth," they strove to liberate language and poetry in particular.[16] Indeed, Jacques Baron has argued that the subject of Tzara's plays is really the birth of language via the destruction and reconstruction of the word.[17] Thus, the Dada poets wished to stimulate thought and to achieve new states of consciousness by manipulating their (verbal) medium. The key concept in this context, one that counterbalances the principle of scandal, is that of spontaneity. Both tenets derive from the fanatical devotion to freedom that characterizes the Dada adventure. Just as the Dadaists were interested in the activity of the mind, their preoccupation with spontaneity and the gratuitous reflects their interest in the prelogical existence of experience and thought. Trying to grasp our being in its primitive coherence (or incoherence), they sought to embrace absolute psychological reality.

Once one manages to overcome the initial impression of raving nonsense, Dada is remarkable for the freshness and vigor of its compositions. As I have tried to show, there is an immense *joie de vivre* connected with the life and art of its practitioners, which by itself is enough to refute the charges of nihilism that one still encounters. Above all,

15. Cited in Rudolf Arnheim, *The Genesis of a Painting: Picasso's Guernica* (Berkeley: University of California Press, 1962), 13.
16. Tristan Tzara, "Dada manifeste sur l'amour faible et l'amour amer," in *Oeuvres complètes*, ed. Henri Béhar (Paris: Flammarion, 1975), 1: 379.
17. Jacques Baron, *L'An 1 du surréalisme* and *L'An dernier* (Paris: Denoël, 1969), 141, cited in Matthews, *Theatre in Dada and Surrealism*, 19.

the Dadaists stressed the importance of play as a path to liberation. Although their poetry is necessarily verbal, it communicates largely on a nonverbal level in terms of images, emotions, rhythms, and so forth. Opposing discursive and nondiscursive structures to each other, the Dadaists were among the first to discover that words could be used to convey information that was essentially extralinguistic. Dada deserves to be recognized for releasing this knowledge, this energy, which as we have seen is at the very core of the creative experience, and for making it available to generations of writers to come. Hopefully, readers of the present anthology will experience some of that same energy as they shop for interesting poems in *The Dada Market*.

Readers who are already familiar with the Dada movement may be surprised at some of the principles that have guided the selection and organization of the following texts. Scholars in particular will no doubt regret the absence of a critical apparatus, historical observations, and an extensive bibliography. However, since the anthology was conceived as a joyful experience rather than as a scholarly presentation, I have adopted a more streamlined approach. Above all, I would like the reader to approach the poems in the spirit in which they were originally written— for the sheer pleasure of it. Readers who want to learn more about Dada experiments with language will find a brief bibliography at the end. Possessing few critical or historical pretentions, this anthology is intended primarily as an introduction to Dada poetry. Toward this end, I have chosen examples of the most important kinds of poems from individuals writing in a variety of languages. Within the existing space limitations, I have tried to represent a maximum number of poets with a couple of fine but typical pieces. Although the anthology does not attempt to provide complete coverage, it singles out the more important and/or representative members of the various groups. Regretfully, I was unable to obtain permission to include works by Aragon. In addition, some of the more exotic manifestations, such as Polish Dada or Hungarian Dada, have had to be excluded due to my lack of linguistic competence. In any case, although their experiments are undeniably interesting, these groups were situated on the movement's periphery. By contrast those included in the present volume were more centrally located and played a direct role in Dada's evolution.

As literary historians have long acknowledged, Dada was the first movement to emerge during the twentieth century that was truly international in scope. Notwithstanding this fact, literary histories invariably divide the Dadaists into groups according to their geographical location and analyze their accomplishments accordingly. In order to avoid categorizing the poets included in this anthology by their country of origin, therefore, I have decided to list them in alphabetical order. Had they been organized according to the geographical model, Zurich, Berlin, and Paris Dada would have dwarfed the other centers by comparison. Thus, I have sought to stress the movement's international character by playing down the poets' national origins. It is not a question of promoting some centers as equally important to others but simply of giving them all equal exposure. Indeed, by removing each poet from his or her particular group, I am forcing each one to justify his or her poetry independently. Each poem must stand or fall according to its own merits and by comparison with the other poems in the book. Arranging the texts alphabetically by author seems to be a good way to avoid any sort of bias. I would like readers to decide for themselves whether an individual poet is any good or not. I also hope they will consider what the various writers have in common despite the national and linguistic differences that separate them. As the compositions stand, they are carefully balanced by language area and reflect Dada's impressive linguistic diversity. I have considered not the number of poems per poet but rather the length of his or her total contribution, keeping the idea of a bilingual format continually in mind. Except for the more important figures, I have restricted each author to the same approximate number of lines. However, since poets writing in French and German were more numerous and since they played a disproportionate role in the movement, they occupy approximately half the anthology. Each of the remaining languages (English, Spanish, Italian, Catalan, and Dutch) receives an equal amount of space.

Although the poems' titles have been regularized throughout, I have reproduced the original texts as accurately as possible. To a certain extent, I suppose I have tended to choose works that are translatable. Of necessity, some of the wilder intermedia experiments have been excluded such as film and poetry, simultaneous poetry, number poems, performance poetry, and so forth. By and large, since these works resist translation, there is little point in including them in an anthology such as this. However fascinating they may be to specialists, moreover, many of them are rather boring. The following example, composed by Picabia, will demonstrate what I mean:

$$
\begin{array}{r}
4967018 \\
5384321 \\
6423095 \\
\underline{1938776} \\
18713210 \\
\underline{6000} \\
9210 \\
\underline{0000} \\
9210
\end{array}
$$

Although I have included examples of purely visual and purely auditory poetry, there are limits to every reader's patience. In addition, many of the intermedia efforts do not lend themselves to the present format but are (or were) directed at a theater audience.

As one might expect, the level of accomplishment varies from one poet to the next and even from poem to poem. It should come as no surprise that the Dadaists were not uniformly brilliant and that they were capable of writing poetry that was less than perfect. Instead of choosing the very best works they produced, which would have given a false impression of the movement, I have preferred to present a cross section. As the reader will discover, some of the poets were truly revolutionary, and others were less extreme in their desire to break with tradition. Accordingly, some of the poems constitute a radical critique of poetic language and form, while others attempt less ambitious reforms. In the best poems, one encounters a critique of language itself and an attempt to deconstruct the cultural sign system. More than anything, I have included works that I think are interesting, that will appeal to the reader on one or more levels. I also hope that readers who possess the requisite language skills will attempt to decipher the original poems and compare them with my own versions. However, the real subject of *The Dada Market* is not translation but poetry. More precisely, the volume is concerned with exploring the possibilities of the poetic act and its social, semiotic, and aesthetic ramifications. The real heroes of this book are the Dadaists themselves, who included some amazingly creative people.

THE DADA MARKET

Marius de Zayas, *Portrait of José Juan Tablada*
(Courtesy of Rodrigo de Zayas).

Pierre Albert-Birot

Pierre Albert-Birot (1885–1967) was the editor of a journal entitled *SIC* (*Sons, Idées, Couleurs*), which appeared in Paris from 1916 to 1919. A friend and disciple of Guillaume Apollinaire, whose landmark play *Les Mamelles de Tirésias* he produced single-handedly, Birot was a man of many talents. An active playwright, painter, and set designer, he also authored quite a few volumes of poetry. Although his poems drew on many sources, they were faithful to the Dada spirit on numerous occasions.

Rasoir mécanique

Couchez vous sur le dos et comptez les feuilles des arbres
          DANS LA FORÊT UNE A UNE
          LES JEUNES FILLES ONT PASSÉ
Splendeur des mondes verts unis aux mondes bleus
       i i   i i i i i i i   i
Forêts des elephantslionstigresserpentsetjaguars
Vous êtes quelque part
Cependant que je rêve à Clamart
Forêts d'Asie UNE NOISETTE et des deux Amériques
               PIGEON VOLE
               AVION VOLE
               PLOMB VOLE
     HI HI HI HI HI   HA HA HA HA HA
Incommensurabilité
De notre éternité
Blancheur et bleuité
          MARIE VIENS VOIR
De l'insonorité
Nous irons dans des gares
Et dans des ports
          IL EST PASSÉ PAR ICI
          LE FURET DES BOIS MESDAMES
          IL EST PASSÉ PAR ICI
En bateaux cheminsdefer
A travers
Terresetmers
               IL VA PLEUVOIR
Pour voir

Mechanical Razor

Lie on your back and count the leaves on the trees
      IN THE FOREST ONE BY ONE
      THE GIRLS PASSED BY
Splendor of green worlds united to blue worlds
    i i   i i i i i i i   i
Forests of elephantslionstigerssnakesandjaguars
You are somewhere
While i dream at Clamart
Forests of Asia A HAZEL-NUT and of both Americas
        PIGEON FLIES
        PLANE FLIES
        LEAD FLIES
  HI HI HI HI HI   HA HA HA HA HA
Incommensurability
Of our eternity
Whiteness and bluishness
      MARIE COME SEE
Of the absence of sound
We will go into railroad stations
And into ports
    HE CAME THROUGH HERE
    THE WILD FERRET LADIES
    HE CAME THROUGH HERE
In ships railroadtrains
Across
Landsandseas
      IT IS GOING TO RAIN
To see

La Joie des sept couleurs
(fragment)

C'est un homme enfermé dans une projection
Inutile de lui demander le nom de la rue où il est
Elles sont deux mais il n'y en a qu'une
A bientôt nous sommes encore ici peut-être pour
Redoutablepossibilitédeschosesquinesontpasencor
Kac Kec Kic koc kuc kac kec kic kac
Un sourire a passé entouré de dentelles
Nous ne marchons jamais dans le même sens
C'est pourquoi je dis nous nous rencontrerons
Il y a des gens qui passent dans la projection
Et qui ne sont pas éclairés cor cor encor accord
Sous les sons les sons sont saouls suçons
Personne n'a jamais vu le moteur qui produit la lumière
Ils sont bien obligés de devenir quelquefois inhu-
Mains le petit oiseau mangera le serpent
Noir et blanc le projecteur est sur l'autre trottoir

Catastrophe

La lumière était artificielle les deux sentiments se sont rencontrés comme
deux trains
Puis les soldats indiens sont passés par dessus
Puis la terre a recommencé à rouer
Puis le métro est reparti

The Joy of the Seven Colors
(excerpt)

He is a man enclosed in a picture on the screen
Useless to ask him the name of the street where he is
They are two but there is only one of them
Until later we are still here perhaps for
Formidablepossibilityofthingsthatarenotyet
Kac Kec Kic koc kuc kac kec kic kac
A smile passed by surrounded by lace
We never walk in the same direction
That's why I say we will meet each other
There are people who pass in the picture
And who are not illuminated gain gain again against
With the same sounds the sounds sound sane sow ends
No one has ever seen the motor that produces the light
They are compelled sometimes to become inhu-
Man the tiny bird will eat the snake
Black and white the projector is on the opposite sidewalk

Catastrophe

The light was artificial the two sentiments met like two trains
Then the Indian soldiers passed above
Then the earth began to wheel again
Then the subway left again

Guillaume Apollinaire

Guillaume Apollinaire (1880–1918) championed both experimental poetry and painting, much of which he published in his journal *Les Soirées de Paris*. Despite its Symbolist beginnings, his poetry paved the way for Dada and for Surrealism through its insistence on "surprise" as a legitimate aesthetic principle. In 1914 together with Francis Picabia, Marius de Zayas, and Alberto Savinio, Apollinaire collaborated on a pantomime entitled *A quelle heure un train partira-t-il pour Paris?* Like the latter, a number of his poems embody the Dada spirit perfectly.

0,50

As-tu pris la pièce de dix sous
Je l'ai prise

Chapeau-Tombeau

On a niché
Dans son tombeau
L'oiseau perché
Sur ton chapeau

Il a vécu
En Amérique
Ce petit cul
            Or
Nithologique

            Or
J'en ai assez
Je vais pisser

Un Poème

Il est entré
Il s'est assis
Il ne regarde pas le pyrogène à cheveux rouges
L'allumette flambe
Il est parti

0,50

Did you take the ten-cent piece
I took it

Hat-Tomb

Marooned
On your bonnet
His tomb
There upon it

He came from
Martinique
One dumb
Ex-parakeet

    That's
Enough for me
I'll take a pee

A Poem

He entered the room
He took a seat
He ignored the firebug with red hair
The match flamed
He went away

Walter Conrad Arensberg

Walter Conrad Arensberg (1878–1954) was actively involved with New York Dada, many of whose members congregated at his apartment located at 33 West 67th Street. These included figures such as Francis Picabia, Marcel Duchamp, Juliette Roche, Arthur Cravan, Jean Crotti, Edgar Varèse, Man Ray, and Mina Loy. Independently wealthy, he supported a variety of Dada ventures and acquired a magnificent art collection including some thirty works by Duchamp alone. His poetry appeared in journals such as *Others*, *TNT*, *Rogue*, and *The Blind Man*.

Ing

Ing? Is it possible to mean ing?
Suppose
      for the termination in *g*
                  a disoriented
                  series
      of the simple fractures
                  in sleep.
                  Soporific
      has accordingly a value for soap
                  so present to
                  sew pieces.
                  And *p* says: Peace is.
And suppose the *i*
          to be big in ing
          as Beginning.
                Then Ing is to ing
as aloud
      accompanied by times
and the meaning is a possibility
               of ralsis.

Theorem

For purposes of illusion
                              the actual ascent of two waves
                                    transparent to a basis
                                    which has a disappearance of its own
is timed
          at the angle of incidence
                                          to the swing of a suspended
                                                    lens
from which the waves wash
                              the protective coloration.
Through the resultant exposure
                                    to a temporal process
an emotion
          ideally distant
                              assumes on the uneven surface
                                                    descending
          as the identity to be demonstrated
the three dimensions
                    with which it is incommensurate.

Arithmetical Progression of the Verb "To Be"

On a sheet of paper
                dropped with the intention of demolishing
                space
                by the simple subtraction of a necessary plane
draw a line that leaves the present
                in addition
                carrying forward to the uncounted columns
                            of the spatial ruin
                            now considered as complete
                the remainder of the past.
The act of disappearing
                which in the three-dimensional
                is the fate of the convergent
                        vista
is thus
                under the form of the immediate
arrested in a perfect parallel
                of being
                in part.

Céline Arnauld

Céline Arnauld (1893–1952) published widely in Paris Dada publications such as *Proverbe, Cannibale, Littérature, 391,* and *Z.* Married to the poet Paul Dermée, who directed several influential reviews, she edited a journal called *Projecteur* and was the author of several volumes of poetry and several novels. A second review entitled *M'Amenez-Y* was announced at one point but never materialized.

Entre voleurs

Mais le jeu de l'archet
            sur les trois bougies allumées
magnétise le coffre aux jetons . . .
                  Un gagnant
puis vient une ballade en lambeaux
Le baladin est mort
            au bout de sa chanson

Les Ronge-Bois

Tout près de l'angoisse
les moustiques en folie
Autour de l'ampoule la mort de l'oiseau
Dans l'atmosphère les atomes en oripeaux
                  s'envolant avec la pluie
trainant dans une parade novice
                  des moulures harmoniques
Tandis qu'au pays de Mendoza
les mandores chassent les chevaux de bois
à travers champs
et les grandes roues sont poussées
par des éléphants
Au Collège de France
ils s'endorment sur les bancs

Moi je ne sais rien que maudire
et divaguer contre l'hypothèse . . .

Among Thieves

But the play of the violin bow
                              on the three lighted candles
magnetizes the box of tokens . . .
                              A winner
then there comes a ballad in tatters
The composer died
                    at the end of his song

The Wood-Gnawers

Close by the anguish
the crazed mosquitos
Around the lightbulb the bird's death
In the atmosphere the atoms in cheap finery
                    flying away with the rain
dragging harmonic moldings
                    in a novice parade
While in Mendoza's country
the mandoras chase the wooden horses
across the fields
and the great wheels are pushed
by elephants
At the Collège de France
They fall asleep on the benches

Me I only know how to curse
and ramble on against hypotheses . . .

Avertisseur

Les sentiments
descentes de lit dans la maison
de l'antiquaire
Matin
Les ailes de l'aéroplane
balancent le réveil des amours
en chemin de fer
Les rails en pleurs
l'intelligence déraille
et sans souci les mécaniciens se disputent
les chansons des wagons-lits
Mes amis mes amis
ne vous fiez pas à l'étincelle
le feu prend partout
même dans vos cervelles
Arrêt première station
le chef de gare sans raison
—est-ce l'étalage du soleil
sur les fenêtres du wagon
ou l'inspiration anti-alcool
du matin en papillotes—
divague en jonglant avec les colis
sévèrement remplis de café réveil-matin
La puissance des catapultes
brise les ailes trop fragiles de l'aéroplane
            balançoire de vieilles tendresses
Ohé mes très chers amis
sur les sentiments en descente de lit
le temps passe
la pluie tombe méfiante et mesquine
Vos paroles sont des schrapnells
sur les roues tournesol
Les cimetières s'allongent jusqu'à l'herbe
                              morte...
Prenez garde aux tombes ouvertes

Alarm

Sentiments
getting out of bed in the antiquary's
house
Morning
The airplane's wings
balance the reawakening of loves
on the train
The rails in tears
intelligence derails
and the mechanics vie dispassionately for
the songs of the pullman coaches
My friends my friends
don't trust in sparks
fire erupts everywhere
even in your brains
Stop first station
the crazy station-master
—is it the display of sunlight
on the coach windows
or the anti-alcohol inspiration
of the morning in paper curls—
rambles on while juggling the packages
full to the brim with alarm-clock coffee
The catapults' power
breaks the too fragile wings of the airplane
            see-saw of ancient tendernesses
Hello my very dear friends
time passes
over feelings of getting out of bed
the rain falls suspicious and petty
Your words are shrapnel
on the sunflower wheels
The cemeteries extend to the dead grass...
Watch out for the open graves

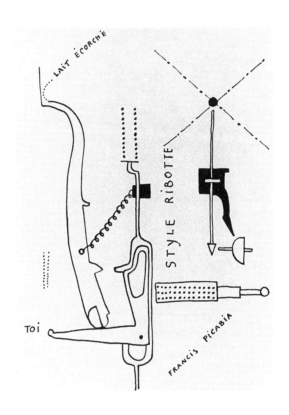

Francis Picabia, *Teeth Come to One's Eyes
Like Tears* (COPYRIGHT 1992 ARS, N.Y. /
SPADEM / ADAGP).

Hans (Jean) Arp

Hans Arp (1886–1966), whose French name was Jean, was one of the truly germinal figures of the Dada movement. Equally at home in poetry and in painting, he published in both German and French and perfected a biomorphic style in art that brought him great fame. A cofounder of the Zurich Dada movement, Arp moved to Cologne in 1919 where he created a similar group with Max Ernst and Johannes Theodor Baargeld. Like Ernst, he eventually migrated to Paris where he continued his Dada activities.

Bim bim . . .

Bim bim ausglim du kurzer kind
Hinfall der
Rot ist der
Rot ist du und du
Also auch der wesenkampf
Also auch der monddudu
Also auch der adlerstall

Wau wau glirrwirrli zirr
Hinfall das
Rot ist das
Rot ist du und du
Also auch das dadahaus
Also auch das muffelohr
Also auch das maskenfleisch

Bim bim ausglim du kurzer kind
Hinfall die
Rot ist die
Rot ist du und du
Also auch die flaschennot
Also auch die Wellenkammer
Also auch die afterlieb

Bim Bim . . .

Bim bim dim down you short child
Collapse of the
Red is the
Red is you and you
So too the struggle for existence
So too the doo-doo moon
So too the eagle stable

Bow-wow glirrwilddli zirr
Collapse of the
Red is the
Red is you and you
So too the dada house
So too the crucible ear
So too the masked meat

Bim bim dim down you short child
Collapse of the
Red is the
Red is you and you
So too the need for bottles
So too the wave chamber
So too anal love

Kaspar ist tot

weh unser guter kaspar ist tot
wer trägt nun die brennende fahne im zopf wer dreht die kaffeemühle
wer lockt das idyllische reh
auf dem meer verwirrte er die schiffe mit dem wörtchen parapluie und
die winde nannte er bienenvater
weh weh weh unser guter kaspar ist tot heiliger bimbam kaspar ist tot
die heufische klappern in den glocken wenn man seinen vornamen
   ausspricht darum seufze ich weiter kaspar kaspar kaspar
warum bist du ein stern geworden oder eine kette aus wasser an einem
   heißen wirbelwind oder ein euter aus schwarzem licht oder ein
   durchsichtiger ziegel an der stöhnenden trommel des felsigen
   wesens
jetzt vertrocknen unsere scheitel und sohlen und die feen liegen
   halbverkohlt auf den scheiterhaufen jetzt donnert hinter der sonne
die schwarze kegelbahn und keiner zieht mehr die kompasse
   und die räder der schiebkarren auf
wer ißt nun mit der ratte am einsamen tisch wer verjagt den teufel wenn
   er die pferde verführen will wer erklärt uns die monogramme in
   den sternen
seine büste wird die kamine aller wahrhaft edlen menschen zieren doch
   das ist kein trost und schnupftabak für einen totenkopf

Kaspar Is Dead

woe our good kaspar is dead
who will bear the burning banner in his pigtail now who will turn the
    coffee grinder
who will entice the idyllic deer
he entangled the ships at sea with the word umbrella and he called the
    wind bee-keeper
woe woe woe our good kaspar is dead dear me kaspar is dead
the hay-fish bells chatter when his name is pronounced so I heave
    another sigh kaspar kaspar kaspar
why have you become a star or a chain of water on a hot whirlwind or
    an udder of black light or a transparent brick on the groaning drum
    of craggy reality
now our crowns and soles are withering away and the fairies lie half-
    charred at the funeral pyre
    now the black bowling alley
thunders behind the sun and no one winds the compasses and the
    wheelbarrow wheels any more
who will eat at the lonely table now with the rat who will expel the devil
    when he tries to entice the horses who will interpret the stars'
    monograms for us
his bust will adorn the mantels of all truly noble men but that is no
    consolation and snuff for a death's-head

Johannes Baader

Johannes Baader (1875–1955) actively participated in the Berlin movement from 1918 to 1920, together with his friend Raoul Hausmann. Quickly assuming the title of Oberdada (Supreme Dada), he engaged in so many iconoclastic activities that his colleagues proclaimed him president of the world. Among other things, he contributed to *Der Dada* and *Dada Almanach* and interrupted the proceedings of the inaugural session of the Weimar Republic to nominate himself for president.

Fifi

Maßreparatur speziell Rahmenarbeit . . . Fifi legt 16 Eier in den grünen Rinnstein. Nicht Einstein. O du grüner Rinnstein! Wirst du die 16 Eier ausbrüten? Bitte, bitte, sagt Fifi.

Es ist grüner Dotter in meinen grünen Eiern. Und die Kücken haben grüne Glasaugen.

Fifi, warum nimmst du grüne, und nicht rote Grütze ins Haarwasser?

Aber Fifi hört nicht und sieht nicht. Sie denkt immer noch an den Rinnstein und seine grünen Glotzaugen.

Was hast du für einen großen Mund, süßer Rinnstein! Meine Kücken werden Schlagsahne essen. Ich, Fifi, werde sie kochen. Grün kochen. Es ist alles grün, was gelb ist. Fifi ist blau vor Freude.

Werde doch blau, grüner Rinnstein! Meine Kücken wollen lieber blau fressen.

Fifi ist verrückt geworden. Fifi will nur noch grüne Kücken braten. Fifi.

Maßreparatur, speziell Rahmenarbeit, singt Fifi und pfeift dazu mit ihren blaugeränderten Fußnägeln. Fifis grüne Blauaugen blitzen gelb durch den resedablanken Rinnstein.

Fifi will sich Stiefel anmessen auf der Nord-Südbahn. Fifi kauft braune Billets für ihre 16 roten Kücken und geht die Strecke ab. 400 Millionen kostet die Nordsüdbahn und früher nur 32. Fifi nimmt den grünen Rinnstein unter den Arm, setzt sich ins Gras und singt das graue Lied von der Nordsüdbahn:

O Fifi soda, fifi, fifi, fifi, ffa, ffa. O Fifi soda, fifi, fifi,

ffa, ffi, ffa, fifi, ffa, fifi, ffa.

Komm, grüner Rinnstein, setz dich in die Nordsüdbahn. Und dann

verschieben wir meine 16 Kücken: eines für siebzehn, eines für

fünfzehn, eines für vierzehn Milliarden rote Grütze.

Fifi

Measured repair special structural work . . . Fifi puts 16 eggs in the green drain. Not the train. Oh you green drain! Will you hatch the 16 eggs? Please, please, says Fifi.

There are green yolks in my green eggs. And the chicks have green glass eyes.

Fifi, why do you use green, and not red grits in your hair lotion?

But Fifi is not listening or observing. She is still thinking about the drain and its green goggle-eyes.

What a large mouth you have, sweet drain! My chicks will eat whipped cream. I, Fifi, will cook them. Cook green. All is green that is yellow. Fifi is blue from pleasure.

So become blue, green drain! My chicks want to eat dear blue.

Fifi has gone crazy. Fifi still only wants to roast green chicks. Fifi.

Measured repair special structural work, sings Fifi and whistles too with her toenails which have turned blue. Fifi's blue eyes are green and flash yellow through the bright mignonette drain.

Fifi wants to be measured for boots on the North-South train. Fifi buys brown tickets for her 16 red chicks and leaves the track. The North-South train costs 400 million and earlier only 32. Fifi puts the green drain under her arm, sits in the grass, and sings the gray song of the North-South train:

O Fifi soda, fifi, fifi, fifi, ffa, ffa. O Fifi soda, fifi, fifi,

ffa, ffi, ffa, fifi, ffa, fifi, ffa.

Come green drain, sit in the North-South train. And then let's

sell my 16 chicks on the black-market: one for seventeen, one

for fifteen, one for fourteen billion red grits.

Johannes Theodor Baargeld

Johannes Theodor Baargeld (1892–1927) was a member of the Cologne Dadas, together with Max Ernst and Hans (Jean) Arp. In addition to contributing both poems and paintings to the movement, he edited a procommunist review entitled *Der Ventilator* and coedited *Bulletin D*, *Dada W/3*, and *Die Schammade*. Among other things, he collaborated with Ernst on some of the collages included in the latter's Fatagaga series.

Bimbamresonnanz 1

Stutzflügelalwa schlägt die flügelfeder
schlägt alwa stutzuhr bimbamresonnanz
Breschkowska-revolution der großmütter schlägt die
    augenleder
und ihren kalzionierten Jordanwasserschwanz
alwa pissoirgeläute brütet stutzige Landeseier
Ländnerin herien und hierin alwe
doch verbimmeltes pedal toniert schon alwenweiher
flügeluhr schlägt bim auf ländnermalve
breschkowskaja schlägt die Lederdrüse
bis die muttermöndchen bimmeln schöpfersalbe
Und des Ewigen scheerenfernrohr überkrebst als
    alwe
Bimmelnd toten alwa landgemüse

Bimmelresonnanz II

Bergamotten faltern im Petroleumhimmel
Schwademasten asten Schwanenkerzen
Teleplastisch starrt das Cherimbien Gewimmel
In die überöffneten Portierenherzen
Inhastiert die Himmelbimmel
Feldpostbrief recochettiert aus Krisenhimmel
Blinder Schläger sternbepitzt sein Queerverlangen
Juste Berling rückt noch jrad die Mutterzangen
Fummelmond und ferngefimmel
Barchenthose flaggt die Kaktusstangen
Lämmergeier zieht die Wäscheleine
Wäschelenden losen hupf und falten
Zigarrinden sudeln auf den Alten
Wettermännchen kratzt an ihrem Beine
Bis alle Bimmeln angehalten

Dingdong Resonance 1

Baby-grand alwa strikes its wing-feather
strikes alwa mantelpiece clock dingdong resonance
Breschkowska-revolution of grandmothers strikes the eye leather
and its calcinated Jordan-water prick
    alwa chiming pissoir incubates startled country eggs
    country women here and within alwe
    yet tinkled pedal sounds quite alwen pond
    wing-clock strikes ding on rustic mallow
        breschkowskaja strikes the leather gland
        until the mama moon tinkling dipper salve
        And Eternity's scissor-telescope troubles itself as alwe
        Tinkling lifeless alwa country vegetables

Tinkling Resonance II

    Citrus trees gather in the petroleum sky
    Rows of masts bear swan candles
    The cherimbian swarm stares teleplastically
    Into the porters' open hearts
    The tinkling sky makes an arrest
Military letter ricochets off unemployment heaven
Blind hitter starbepits his slanting demand
Just Berling still moves jrad the mother forceps
Polished moon and far sledgehammered
Fustian trousers flag the cactus poles
Lamb-fiddler pulls the clothesline
Washing-hips draw lots hop and pleats
Cigar rinds soil the elders
Weather mannequin scratches its legs
Until all tinkling has ceased

Hugo Ball

Hugo Ball (1886–1927) was the guiding light of Zurich Dada, which grew out of his artistic cabaret. Together with his wife Emmy Hennings, Marcel Janco, Tristan Tzara, and Hans (Jean) Arp, he published the review *Cabaret Voltaire* and collaborated on its successor *Dada*. Ball's training was primarily theatrical, and his contribution to the movement was as an actor, a director, and a performer. Often providing musical accompaniment, he specialized in reading "sound poems," dressed in elaborate costumes.

KARAWANE

jolifanto bambla ô falli bambla
grossiga m'pfa habla horem
égiga goramen
higo bloiko russula huju
hollaka hollala
anlogo bung
blago bung
blago bung
bosso fataka
ü üü ü
schampa wulla wussa ólobo
hej tatta gôrem
eschige zunbada
wulubu ssubudu uluw ssubudu
tumba ba- umf
kusagauma
ba - umf

Gadji Beri Bimba

gadji beri bimba glandridi laula lonni cadori
gadjama gramma berida bimbala glandri galassassa laulitalomini
gadji beri bin blassa glassala laula lonni cadorsu sassala bim
gadjama tuffm i zimzalla binban gligla wowolimal bin beri ban
o katalominal rhinozerossola hopsamen laulitalomini hoooo
gadjama rhinozerossola hopsamen
bluku terullala blaulala loooo

zimzim urullala zimzim urullala zimzim zanzibar zimzalla zam
elifantolim brussala bulomen brussala bulomen tromtata
velo da bang bang affalo purzamai affalo purzamai lengado tor
gadjama bimbalo glandridi glassala zingtata pimpalo ögrögöööö
viola laxato viola zimbrabim viola uli paluji malooo

tuffm im zimbrabim negramai bumbalo negramai bumbalo tuffm
    i zim
gadjama bimbala oo beri gadjama gaga di gadjama affalo pinx
gaga di bumbalo bumbalo gadjamen
gaga di bling blong
gaga blung

André Breton

André Breton (1896–1966) is best known as one of the founders of Surrealism, which he headed until his death, but like the other members of the group, he played an important part in Paris Dada and participated in all the important manifestations. Together with Louis Aragon and Philippe Soupault, he published the review *Littérature* and contributed to numerous Dada publications. The author of many poems and critical essays, Breton collaborated with Soupault on *Les Champs magnétiques*, which prepared the way for Surrealism.

Pièce fausse

A Benjamin Péret

Du vase en cristal de Bohème
Du vase en cris
Du vase en cris
Du vase en
En cristal
Du vase en cristal de Bohème
Bohème
Bohème
En cristal de Bohème
Bohème
Bohème
Bohème
Hème hème oui Bohème
Du vase en cristal de Bo Bo
Du vase en cristal de Bohème
Aux bulles qu'enfant tu soufilais
Tu soufflais
Tu soufflais
Flais
Flais
Tu soufflais
Qu'enfant tu soufflais
Du vase en cristal de Bohème
Aux bulles qu'enfant tu soufflais
Tu soufflais
Tu soufflais
Oui qu'enfant tu soufflais
C'est là c'est là tout le poème
Aube éphé
Aube éphé
Aube éphémère de reflets
Aube éphé
Aube éphé
Aube éphémère de reflets

False Piece

For Benjamin Péret

From the crystal vase from Bohemia
From the crys
From the crys
From the
Crystal vase
From the crystal vase from Bohemia
Bohemia
Bohemia
Crystal vase from Bohemia
Bohemia
Bohemia
Bohemia
Hemia hemia yes Bohemia
From the crystal vase from Bo Bo
From the crystal vase from Bohemia
To the bubbles as a child that you blew
That you blew
That you blew
Blew
Blew
That you blew
As a child that you blew
From the crystal vase from Bohemia
To the bubbles as a child that you blew
That you blew
That you blew
Yes as a child that you blew
There you have there you have the whole poem
Ephemeral
Ephemeral
Ephemeral dawn of reflections
Ephemeral
Ephemeral
Ephemeral dawn of reflections

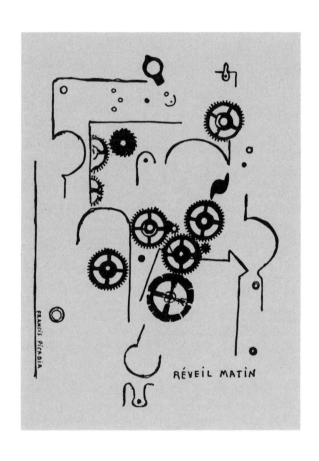

Francis Picabia, *Alarm Clock* (COPY-
RIGHT 1992 ARS, N.Y. / SPADEM / ADAGP).

Til Brugman

Emerging from relative obscurity, Til Brugman (1888–1958) has received more and more attention in recent years. Associated with the Dutch De Stijl group, headed by Theo van Doesburg and Piet Mondrian, she was interested in geometric art, architecture, and design — grouped under the heading of Constructivism — and published in their journal *De Stijl*. Her experiments with permutation and combination in visual poetry make her one of the earliest precursors of the Concrete poetry movement.

R

R   R

    R   R   R

REK   REK

    RAK   RAK   RAK

TREK   TREK

    TRAK   TRAK   TRAK

STREK   STREK

    STRAK   STRAK   STRAK

STREKKEN STREKKEN

STRAK   STRAK   STRAK

STREKKEN

        STRAK

R

R   R
     R   R   R
RECK   RECK
     RACK   RACK   RACK
TREK   TREK
     TRACK   TRACK   TRACK
STREAK   STREAK
     STRUCK STRUCK STRUCK
STRICKEN STRICKEN
STRUCK   STRUCK   STRUCK
STRICKEN
          STRUCK

Gino Cantarelli

Like most of the Italian poets and painters, Gino Cantarelli—who was both—was associated with Futurism for awhile. From 1917 to 1920, he published the journal *Procellaria*, together with Aldo Fiozzi, which combined Futurist and Dadaist tendencies. In 1920 the two editors joined with Julius Evola to publish *Bleu*, which was devoted entirely to Dada and which appeared in Mantua like the earlier journal.

14 heures—soir

Grande symphonie barbare
paysage de l'après-midi

océan de fraicheur   petite ville de province   dans
le viola du coucher   bourgeois à la promenade avec
les petites filles aux jardins délassants . . .
        Poésie   été de soupirs de décadence-Ancien-
nes soies d'argent sur les arbres arides pénombres d'an-
gles rouges et blancs-aïoles de l'Est   veines et nerfs
d'agilité   impossibilité   chaud   chaud encore
        ce soir viendra la lune-tranquille et grande sur
les cubes des maisons   lente sur les rues désertes
où—seule—une nénie lointaine   malade parlera aux
idoles de la nuit. . . .
mais hélas—je vais me promener dans la foule dans
l'électricité   or   mercure   en rêvant
une folie quelconque.

2:00 *P.M.*—*Evening*

Great barbarous symphony
afternoon landscape

ocean of coolness   small provincial town   in
the sunset's viola   bourgeois taking a stroll with
little girls in the refreshing gardens . . .
            Poetry   summer of decadent sighs-Ancient
silver silks on the arid trees penumbras of red
and white angles-Eastern aïolis   veins and nerves
with agility   impossibility   hot   still hot
        this evening the moon will appear-peaceful and
huge above the cubes of the houses   slow above the
deserted streets where—alone—a distant   sick dirge
will address the idols of the night. . . .
but alas—I am going to stroll in the crowd in the
electricity   gold   mercury   dreaming of some
sort of folly.

Lumières de mercure

à Germaine et Pierre Albert-Birot
Voyez les claires façades sur silencieux jardins, au crépuscule matinal:
oh le délice léger et sensuel sous le soleil qui arrose de rubans de cristal
toute la floraison parfumée d'atmosphères—
mais je rêve le coucher de la Lumière : je sentirai la douceur ivre des corps
sanglants des nuages qui noient vers le soir sur les villas de silence
lignes de couleurs au travers des ciels opaques qui enharmonisent avec la
chanson électrique des phares pointillant les tableaux de la plastique
humaine   éternelle
flambeaux verts et jaunes de sons sur les ponts de l'horizon pour donner
un Astre à la nuit
frémissements de délire mortel dans les veines et fièvre des muscles : le
passé voudrait-il vaincre les complexions dynamiques de l'art?

Nous courons au travers de prairies sans frontières sans drapeau :
loin.   aux calmes marécages peut-être, les éclats lumineux de
trichromies qui flamboient les toiles de la conception nuptiale de l'univers
et de l'âme
                    orfèvreries qui brillent parmi les teintes abyssales où se
minéralisent les architectures d'hier
la Ville
                                                    le Soir

les rues qui musiquent l'aujourd'hui
je vais m'évanouir sur soies d'améthiste
et d'argent   les rythmes des tziganes
je vais   aux lèvres   d'une créature étrange
je suis dans ses yeux d'azur   la vie
rien   deux baisers   le pathos charnel.

Mercury Lights

For Germaine and Pierre Albert-Birot

See the bright facades on silent gardens, in the dawn's light:
oh the faint sensual delight beneath the sun which sprinkles with
crystal ribbons all the flowers perfumed with atmospheres—
but I dream the Light's setting: I will feel the sweet intoxication
of the clouds' bloody bodies which flood the silent villas toward
evening   lines of color through opaque skies that harmonize with
the beacons' electric song stippling the paintings of eternal
          human plasticity
green and yellow torches of sounds on the horizon's bridges to give
a Star to the night
quiverings of mortal delirium in one's veins and muscular fever:
would the past like to defeat art's dynamic temperaments?
We run across prairies without borders without flags:
far.   perhaps in the calm swamps, the luminous flashes of trichromic
photographs that blaze the canvases of the nuptial conception
of the universe and the soul
                    jewelry shining among the abyssal hues in which
yesterday's architectures fossilize
the Town

                                        the Evening

the streets that give music to today
I am going to faint on amethyst and silver
silks   gypsy rhythms
I am going   to the lips   of a strange creature
I am in her azure eyes   life
nothing   two kisses   carnal pathos.

Dieux—Lumière

à Paul Dermée

Les avions modèlent l'atmosphère
Et le hibou-Soleil roule au travers de la
Terre idôlatre.

Si pour les cieux lunaires une nocturne cavalcade de nuages nous dicte le roman de l'Air, je voudrais pouvoir vivre le poème des Etoiles.

L'horizon m'a bien chanté—un soir—son éternité : peut-être la nouvelle flute de Pan mourant aux tendresses des nymphes sorties des parfums barbares de la Mer.

J'ai dit que les ailes mécaniques font des architectures ; j'ai vu une basilique d'argent qui se levait dans l'azur et les choeurs hiératiques étaient les frissonnantes hélices-HP.

Les yeux de la jeunesse seront azurs lorsque les vents du sud donneront l'Aube aux jardins d'orient.

Mais pourquoi la lune ne veut-elle pas me faire cadeau de sa mélancolie, si bien le soleil m'a donné sa virilité?

Nous voudrons bien nous évanouir dans l'Infini : les Astres sont le silencieux orchestre des mondes inconnus.

et silence   *silence*
                                                         danse
                                                         des lumières

Gods—Light

For Paul Dermée

The airplanes shape the atmosphere
And the Sun-owl rolls across the
idolatrous Earth.

If for the lunar skies a nocturnal cavalcade of clouds dictates the novel of the
Air to us, I would like to live the poem of the Stars.

The horizon sang to me—one night—its eternity: perhaps Pan's new flute
dying among the tender nymphs risen from the barbarous perfumes of the Sea.

I said that mechanical wings make architectures; I have seen a silver
basilica rising in the azure and the hieratic choirs were its quivering pro-
pellers.

Youth's eyes will be blue when the South wind brings the Dawn to the orien-
tal gardens.

But why doesn't the moon want to present me with its melancholy, since the
sun has given me its virility?

We will want to vanish into the Infinite: the Stars are the silent orchestra of
unknown worlds.

and silence

silence
dancing
lights

Malcolm Cowley

Malcolm Cowley (1898–1989) was a member of the Lost Generation of American writers and painters who gravitated to Paris after World War I. Moving with equal freedom in English- and French-speaking circles, whose exploits he later chronicled in *Exile's Return*, Cowley counted the Dadaists among his friends. "In reading a Dada poem," he explained in the latter volume, "the door of meaning is closed and double-locked; the key is thrown away."

Towards a More Passionate Apprehension of Life and Dedicated to Gorham B. Munson

IT was an arduous task. ¶ The man must be a genius. ¶ He is astute in character. ¶ We went to the museum. ¶ Theory is better than practice. ¶ Do you believe in being ceremonious ceremonious? ¶ Words are the man. ¶ The man is a window or a door. ¶ A battledore or double door. ¶ Out of a door the picador. ¶ The door adores the picador the picador the matador. ¶ The matador adores dormice. ¶ He will stay for lunch.

HE debated a long time on the decision but finally discharged the man because he was disarmed as we discerned later. ¶ He surmounted his intangible difficulties with precision. ¶ His nomination took place after the assassination and the massacre was greater than ever before. ¶ His tuition cost a great deal. ¶ He ventured into the rain but eventually the adventure was a failure.

HE worked with alert accuracy. ¶ Eventually the president's attention was demanded. ¶ Eventually the president's attention was incensed. ¶ It was habitual to have perpetual horror of the creature. ¶ The distinguished man had a distinct disagreement and his disappointment disturbed his perfect composure.

IT is probable that he will be punctual punctual punctual and papa why is the man punctual punctual punctual because he is punctual punctual punctual. ¶ The rain descends. ¶ Gently the rain descends the infinitely gentle rain o rain gently descending and I am bored. ¶ Manifestations are geometrical not ethical.

Theo van Doesburg

Theo van Doesburg (1883–1931) had two passions: Constructivism and Dada. With Piet Mondrian he founded the De Stijl group in Holland and published their journal, also called *De Stijl*. Like his fellow members, he was interested in geometric art, architecture, and design. Under the pseudonym I. K. Bonset, he wrote Dada poetry and published the review *Mecano*, reserving a second pseudonym, Aldo Camini, for his Dada criticism. Together with Til Brugman, van Doesburg's interest in visual permutation makes him a precursor of the Concrete poets.

X-Beelden

'k word doordrongen van de kamer waar de tram doorglijdt
ik heb 'n pet op
orgelklanken
van buitendoormijheen
vallen achter mij kapot
kleine scherven
BLIK BLIK BLIK
en glas
kleine zwarte fietsers
glijden en verdwijnen in mijn beeltenis
+ LICHT^n
de ritsigzieke trilkruin van den boom
versnippert het buitenmij
tot bontgekleurd stof
de zwartewitte waterpalen
4 × HORIZONTAL
ontelbare verticale palen
en ook de hooge
gekromde blauwe
RUIMTE
BEN IK

X-Images

I am penetrated by the room through which the streetcar glides
                    I am wearing a cap
organ notes
from outsidethroughme
fall broken behind me
                    tiny shards
                    TIN TIN TIN
                    and glass
little black cyclists
glide and vanish in my image
                    + LIGHT^n
the hysterically trembling treetop
cuts everything outside me
into variegated bits of dust
the black and white pilings
                    4 × HORIZONTAL
innumerable vertical poles
and also the high
curved blue
            SPACE
            THAT'S ME

RUITER

Stap
Paard
STAP
PAARD
Stap
Paard.
STAPPE   PAARD
STAPPE   PAARD
STAPPE   PAARD
STAPPE PAARD   STAPPE PAARD
STEPPE PAARD   STEPPE PAARD
STEPPE PAARD   STEPPE PAARD
STIPPE PAARD STIPPE PAARD STIPPE PAARD
STIP   PAARD
STIP   PAARD
STIP
WOLK

RIDER

Step
Horse
STEP
HORSE
Step
Horse.
STEPPING   HORSE
STEPPING   HORSE
STEPPING   HORSE
stepping horse   stepping horse
stopping horse   stopping horse
stopping horse   stopping horse
stooping horse stooping   horse stooping horse
STOOP   HORSE
STOOP   HORSE
STOOP
CLOUD

X-Beelden (1920)

hé   hé   hé
hebt gij 't lichaamlijk ervaren
hebt gij 't lichaamlijk ervaren
hebt gij 't li **CHAAM** lijk er **VA** ren

Oⁿ

—ruimte en
—tijd
verleden heden toekomst
het achterhierenginds
het doorelkaar van 't niet en de verschijning

kleine verfrommelde almanak
die men ondersteboven leest
MIJN KLOK STAAT STIL

uitgekauwd sigaretteeindie op't
WITTE SERVET

vochtig bruin
ontbinding
GEEST
346   VRACHT AU TO MO BIEL

DWARS

trillend   onvruchtbaar   middelpunt
caricatuur der zwaarte
uomo electrico
rose en grauw en diep wijnrood
de scherven van de kosmos vind ik in m'n thee

Aanteekning: Oⁿ: te lezen nulⁿ; —ruimte en— tijd: te lezen min ruimte
en min tijd.

X-Images (1920)

hey   hey   hey
have you experienced it physically
have you experienced it physically
have you ex**PER**ienced it **PHYS**ically

O^n

—space and
—time
past present future
the behindhereandthere
the confusion of nothingness and appearance
little crumpled almanac
that one reads upside down
MY CLOCK STANDS STILL

   chewed-up cigarette butt on the
WHITE NAPKIN

moist brown
decomposition
SPIRIT
346   **TRUCK TO HAUL FREIGHT**

SLANTING   trembling   sterile   center

caricature of gravity
electric man
            pink and gray and deep wine-red
I find splinters of the cosmos in my tea

N.B. O^n should be read as "zero^n"; —*space* and —*time* should be read as
"minus space" and "minus time."

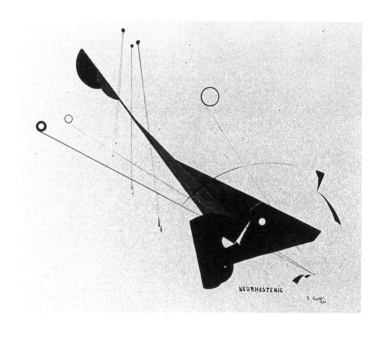

Jean Crotti, *Neurhastenia* (COPYRIGHT 1992 ARS, N.Y. / ADAGP).

Joaquín Edwards Bello

Although born and raised in Chile where he lived most of his life, Joaquín Edwards Bello (1887–1968) was educated in England and spent much time on the continent. Known to his European colleagues as Jacques Edwards, he participated in both the French and the Spanish avant-gardes before becoming one of the innumerable "presidents" of Dada. A prolific novelist who became well known in his own country, he defined Dada in *Metamorfosis* as "an astronomical brew, oblong, somewhat gaseous, and yellow in color."

La guerra

(Notas de un "métèque")

El Kaiser no podía cohabitar más. Esa fue la causa única de la guerra europea. Durante seis meses un aluvión de gigantes hizo temblar los villorrios—*Die Wacht am Rhein*—R Rr Rrr Rrrr Rrrrr. . . . . Los alemanes dicen todo lo que piensan, como los locos. Bolivia y Perú protestan enérgicamente—Un gramófono sobre la Torre Eiffel grita: Bárbaro, Bárbaro, Bárbaro.

—El cisne acorazado muere sin cantar. Los lunáticos toman las trincheras por figuras geométricas. Von Tirpitz torpedeó el Tango. Se moviliza un millón de peluqueros. Sobre los bulevares se erige una estatua al inventor de la quinina. Las francesas se casan con los soldados ingleses porque éstos se lavan los dientes. *Tipperary five o'clock tea Paris rit*. Todos los extranjeros son espías. ¡Cochino neutro! Mi ficha pesa tres kilos y medio en la comisaría del quinto distrito. El sombrero de copa de Poincaré está lleno de piojos. Italia se ha decidido finalmente porque el restaurant Poccardi, del bulevar está lleno de banderas. Acabo de ser fusilado tres veces por culpa de mi cerillera. América compra la guerra. El cambio baja; pero a mí me tiene sin cuidado, porque yo jamás cambio nada.

The War

(Notes by a "spic")
The Kaiser was no longer able to make love. This was the sole
cause of the European war. For six months a spate of giants caused the
miserable towns to tremble—*The Watch on the Rhine*—R Rr Rrr Rrrr
Rrrrr. . . . . Germans say whatever pops into their heads, like madmen.
Bolivia and Peru are protesting energetically. —A gramophone on the
Eiffel Tower cries: "Barbarian, Barbarian, Barbarian."
　　—The armored swan dies without singing. Lunatics mistake the
trenches for geometrical figures. Von Tirpitz has torpedoed the Tango. A
million barbers are being mobilized. A statue to the inventor of quinine
is being erected on the boulevards. The French girls are marrying En-
glish soldiers because they brush their teeth. *Tipperary five o'clock tea pure
Harry*. Every foreigner is a spy. Neutral swine! My file at the police sta-
tion in the 5th arrondissement weighs eight pounds. Poincaré's tophat is
full of lice. Italy has finally made up her mind, since the Poccardi restau-
rant on the boulevard is filled with flags. A firing squad has just exe-
cuted me for the third time because of my matchbox. America is buying
the war. The rate of exchange is dropping; but that doesn't bother me,
since I never change a bit.

Paul Eluard

Like his fellow Surrealists, Paul Eluard (1895–1952) served an apprentice-ship among the Parisian Dadaists. A major figure in both Dada and Surrealism, he was part of the group associated with *Littérature* and participated in all their activities. A prolific poet, Eluard also edited a review entitled *Proverbe*. His poems appeared in a wide range of Dada periodicals, and many of his books of poetry were published in collaboration with Dada artists.

Max Ernst

Dans un coin l'inceste agile
Tourne autour de la virginité d'une petite robe
Dans un coin le ciel délivré
Aux épines de l'orage laisse des boules blanches.

Dans un coin plus clair de tous les yeux
On attend les poissons d'angoisse.
Dans un coin la voiture de verdure de l'été
Immobile glorieuse et pour toujours.

A la lueur de la jeunesse
Des lampes allumées très tard
La première montre ses seins que tuent des insectes
rouges.

La Grande Maison inhabitable

Au milieu d'une ile étonnante
Que ses membres traversent
Elle vit d'un monde ébloui.

La chair que l'on montre aux curieux
Attend là comme les récoltes
La chute sur les rives.

En attendant pour voir plus loin
Les yeux plus grands ouverts sous le vent de ses mains
Elle imagine que l'horizon a pour elle dénoué sa
ceinture.

Max Ernst

In a corner the agile incest
Turns about the virginity of a small dress
In a corner the sky delivered
To the storm's spines leaves white balls.

In a corner brighter with all the eyes
They await the fish of anguish.
In a corner the car of summer greenery
Immobile glorious and eternal.

In the glimmer of youth
Lamps shining very late
The first displays its breasts which red insects kill.

The Great Uninhabitable House

In the middle of an astonishing island
Which her limbs traverse
She lives with a dazzled world.

The flesh that is displayed to the curious
Awaits the waterfall on the shores
Like the harvests.

Awaiting further revelations
Her larger eyes opened beneath the wind of her hands
She imagines the horizon has unbuckled its belt for her.

Max Ernst

Max Ernst (1891–1976) was a cofounder of Cologne Dada with Johannes Baargeld and Hans (Jean) Arp. In addition to contributing both poems and paintings to the movement, he coedited journals entitled *Die Scham-made, Bulletin D,* and *Dada W/3.* His Fatagaga series of photocollages was created in collaboration with his two colleagues. In 1921 he was refused a German passport because of his Dada activities, including the notorious Vorfrühling exhibition that was closed by the police. Ernst eventually settled in Paris where he was active in both Dada and Surrealism.

Die ungeschlagene Fustanella

Wunschgemäss gestatte ich ihnen hiermit, die 56 verwitterungsstufen vom trischen gestein zum sechsblättrigen reliefröslein mit goethes mineralischem nadilass aufzufüllen. Die quer- und längslinien ihrer parallelogramme laufen sodann gleich. Häkeln sie einen ringmeter luft einmal als ersatz eines stäbchens einmal als aufschlitz ihres porphyr lapislazuli und sie werden sich allen anordnungen ihres p. t. herrn direktors ungebrochenen herzens fügen können. Die dritte und vierte reihe wiederholt man noch zweimal, damit die blättchen sich hübsch wundern. Die meisterwerke ihrer konditorei müssen recht scharf gepolstert werden. Sodann spritzen sie ruhig weiter mit gneis, glimmerschiefer und grauwacke und vergessen sie ja nicht, ihre sechs wölbungen mit stalaktit als blätterteig zu steppen.

Die Wasserprobe

Hierbei wird die Faust geballt
Dass der frosch zu boden knallt
Hier die magd die motten putzt
Dass der wind die dämpfe stutzt

Hierbei wird ein dampf verschluckt
Dass der greise bammel zuckt
Dass der warmen fische ei
Knall und fall ins einerlei

The Unwrapped Fustanella

Pursuant to your demand, I hereby permit you to replenish the 56 stages of decomposition of new rock in the hexaphyllous embossed rose with Goethe's mineral remains. The tranverse and the straight lines of your parallelogram thus extend equally. Attach a ring-meter air first as a bacillus substitute, then as an aperture for your porphyry lapis lazuli, and you will understand how to accommodate yourself to all the regulations of your *pro tem* director's unbroken heart. The third and fourth series must be repeated twice until the thin leaf becomes beautifully astonishing. Your bakery's masterpieces must be quite sharply upholstered. Next quietly continue to spray with gneiss, micaceous schist, and graywacke, and remember to quilt your six arches with stalactites as puff pastry.

The Water Torture

Now the fist is clenched
That the firecracker explodes on the ground
Now the maid scours the moths
That the wind trims the fumes

Now a vapor is swallowed
That the old man twitches in a funk
That the warm fish egg
Suddenly falls into monotony

Der alte Vivisektor

Dort auf jenem hügel, so rief der general, sehe ich dichte schützenlinien. Warum werden sie mir nicht gemeldet?
Es sind puppenräuber und blütenstände, wandte der adjutant ein.
Und jene artilleriebeobachtungsstände da drüben?
Das sind die brutknospen auf ihren leitern.
Halblinks ist eine starke batterie von anscheinend grossem kaliber, fragte der führer nochmals; solche führen wir doch nicht.
Ew. Exzellenz haben ganz recht; es sind die bauchteile der eizellen, die spitzengänger der zukunft, die gliedmassen der im schnee begrabenen. Sie übertreffen die sporen an schönheit und klarheit. Sie sind mit wurzelhaaren dicht besetzt. Ihre halskanäle tragen feine wimpern. Die giftzähne verbergen sie in den weichteilen ihrer frauen. Atemöffung und assimilationsfäden tausendfach. Auf dem grunde des bechers der sonnentau.
Vorwärts, antwortete dieser. Die schrumpfung der wandzelle. Das auskeimen der sporen. Die unverbesserliche trinkerin.

The Old Vivisector

There on that hill, the general cried, I see thick lines of skirmishers.
Why haven't they been reported to me?
They are ground beetles and varieties of inflorescence, the adjutant
replied.
And those artillery observation-posts over there?
Those are the brood gemmules on their scales.
To the left there is a powerful battery which seems to have a large
caliber gun, the commander remarked again; we don't have anything
like that ourselves.
Your Eternal Excellency is entirely correct; they are the abdominal
sections of the ooblasts, the vanguard of the future, the limbs of
those buried in the snow. They surpass the spores in beauty and in
clarity. They are densely covered with root hairs. Their neck canals
bear fine cilia. The poison fangs are concealed in their wives' soft
parts. Stoma and assimilation filaments a thousandfold. At the
bottom of the crater is the sundew.
Forward, the other replied. Stricture of the septum cell. Germination
of the spores. The incorrigible drunkard.

Julius Evola

Julius Evola (1898–1974) was an abstract artist, poet, and philosopher who left the Futurist camp to devote himself to Italian Dada. With Gino Cantarelli and Aldo Fiozzi he founded *Bleu* in 1920, which was published in Mantua, and sought to further the Dada cause. Situated in Rome, he contributed to publications such as *Dada* and *Mecano*. In 1920 Evola published *Arte astratta*, which contains examples of his paintings, many of his poems, and a section devoted to theory.

La Fibre s'enflamme et les Pyramides
(très vite)

aeaeaeaeaea eda   s'éclairent les digues verticales   ledah ega
les torpilleurs aux   fontaines   ne touchez pas
sous l'orage extrarose   mourir mourir   les ancres
les soeurs grises et les philosophes sur l'ultratlantique les coupoles
                                        oegooraaa   crépuscule
derrière la pastel les perforatrices les perforatrices
hhhaa   il a signé le quadruple
bregan   aeaeaeaeaeaaaa

The Fiber Catches Fire and the Pyramids
(very quickly)

aeaeaeaeaea eda   the vertical dikes   light up   ledah ega
the torpedo boats with the   fountains   don't touch
beneath the extrapink storm   dying dying   the anchors
the tipsy sisters and the philosophers on the oceanliner the domes
oegooraaa   dusk
behind the crayon the drilling-machines the drilling-machines
hhhaa   he signed the quadruple
bregan   aeaeaeaeaeaaaa

Dada paesaggio

gdâaaara la fiamma nera sciacqua il secondo cielo
                              gd gdâaara
fuori
l'oro scoppia mitragliatrice—sull'orlo iperradio
vulcano morire sdea ea eda—più—l'alfa balla
e le metropoli
        efdd   efdedddea   s   k   rrrrrrrrrrrr   âaaaaa
egli ride
crolla il ponte saracinesca scendeva l'acciaio scende
                      l'acciaio morire rovente
la logica scoppia e la crosta oceano bianco rrrrrrrrr
vibrante atlantide si spezza
                        rrr
le dreadnoughts sotto le serre
si precipita sulla cassaforte turbina etere sahib morire
egli non sa che ore sono
acido lucentissimo ha succhiato il cervello e il
                              potenziale
e gli occhi si sono aperti per la prima volta 417
le salve scrosciano e gli organi control i deliri
entrate ve ne prego   egli ride egli ride
la centrale impazzisce in calcestruzzo
      gz   zzzd   g   m   krrr
              raga blanga
                  râaaaga blanca   hhhhr
aaaaaaaaaaaaaaaaaaaaaaaa
donna logaritmo obice (certamente, si) alluvione
                  § 2 sasso
e la gioia e la morte di tutto questo
al gran serpe Ea
meriggio
                    rrrrrrrrrrrrrrrrrrrrrrrr

Dada Landscape

gdâaaara the black flame rinses the second sky
                              gd gdâaara
outside
the gold explodes machinegun — on the edge hyper-radium
volcano dying sdea ea eda — plus — the alpha bale
and the metropolises
          efdd   efdedddea   s   k   rrrrrrrrrrrr   âaaaaa
he laughs
the bridge collapses portcullis was descending the steel descends
                                        steel dying red-hot
the logic explodes and the crust white ocean rrrrrrrrr
vibrant atlantis breaks up
                    rrr
the dreadnoughts beneath the greenhouses
he hurls himself on the safe turbine ether sahib dying
he doesn't know what time it is
dazzling acid has sucked his brain and his potential
and his eyes have opened for the first time 417
the salvos roar and the organs against delirium
please enter   he laughs he laughs
the central office goes crazy in concrete
          gz   zzzd   g   m   krrr
                    raga blanga
                              râaaaga blanca   hhhhr
aaaaaaaaaaaaaaaaaaaaaaaa
lady logarithm howitzer (certainly, yes) deluge
                              § 2 stone
and the joy and the death of all this
to the great serpent Ea
midday
                    rrrrrrrrrrrrrrrrrrrrrrrr

Respiro

La neve cade negli ambulatori di gomma calda   rondò di
pavoni, o ovattamento d'atmosfera d'ospedale   i grandi acquari in
bagno maria—Pei corridoi del parco non vi è nesssuno
    Una sera lunare porteremo agli artici: si videro ieri i dondolanti
passaggi dei marinai infermi   Due occhi immensi si spalancavano un
istante finestre   ma non spereremo l'azzurro. La vita legnosa fra le
gibbosità di stufe—quando le mani finalmente toccheranno i nuclei ar-
denti in questo deserto pneumatico (due acciai si lanciano nel cielo)
    Passeranno duecento anni   In vetrate bianche si esaurisce l'ara-
besco, ed invariabilmente quella vita di formule nel cloroformio
Ricordo i pesci nel gran vaso di spirito—fra la materia era stata dimen-
ticata di certo un'attesa noncurante : la pioggia calda sulle monache: ora
le due presso ai termosifoni dell'Hotel ed un sorriso pallido cade sulla
pelliccia
    "Wien, nur dich!" In una grande noia sospesa fra le nebbie, incur-
abilmente si sveste di seta una canzone
    Incurabilmente d'ovatta gialla il respiro nelle corsie
    Una rosa inclinata   corsie
    Un'ora
                            incurabilmente nelle corsie
                            la neve

Breath

The snow falls in the hot rubber surgeries   peacock rondeau, or hospital atmosphere stuffing   the large aquariums in waterbaths— There is no one in the park's corridors

One moonlit evening we will take to the arctic: the sick sailors' rolling voyages met yesterday   Two immense eyes opened wide a moment windows   but we will not hope for the blue. The woody life among the stoves' convexity—when the hands finally touch the fiery nuclei in this pneumatic desert (two steels fling themselves into the sky)

Two hundred years will pass   The arabesque exhausts itself in the white windows, and invariably that life of formulas in the chloroform I remember the fish in the large jar of alcohol—among the material a careless expectation has certainly been neglected: the warm rain on the nuns: now the two near the Hotel radiators and a pale smile falls on the fur coat

"Vienna, only you!" In a great weariness suspended between the fogs, a silk song undresses itself incurably

Incurably the breath in the hospital wards with yellow stuffing

A nodding rose   hospital wards

One hour

incurably in the hospital wards
the snow

Marcel Janco, woodcut
(COPYRIGHT 1992 ARS,
N.Y. / ADAGP).

Elsa von Freytag-Loringhoven

The Baroness Elsa von Freytag-Loringhoven (1874–1927) was a legend in her own time. Born and raised in Germany, she immigrated to the United States before World War I and became affiliated with New York Dada. Specializing in outrageous behavior and junk sculpture, with which she adorned her body, she turned her life into a Dada monument. Her poetry appeared in *The Little Review* and in *New York Dada*, which also included a photo of her in the nude.

Affectionate

Wheels are growing on rose-bushes
gray and affectionate
O Jonathan—Jonathan—dear
Did some swallow Prendergast's silverheels—
be drunk forever and more
—with lemon appendicitis?

Holy Skirts

Thought about holy skirts—to tune of "*Wheels are growing on rose-bushes.*" Beneath immovable—carved skirt of forbidding sexlessness—over pavement shoving—gliding—nuns have wheels.

Undisputedly! since—beneath skirts—they are not human! Kept carefully empty cars—running over religious track—local—express—according to velocity of holiness through pious steam—up to heaven!

What for—
what do they unload there—
why do they run?

Senseless wicked expense on earth's provisions—pious idleness—all idleness unless idleness *before action—idleness of youth!*

Start action upstairs—he?
How able do that—all of sudden—when on earth—machinery insufficient—weak—unable to carry—virtuous?

Virtue: stagnation.
Stagnation: absent contents—lifeblood—courage—action! action-n!

Why here?
What here for—?
    To good? ah—!? hurry—speed up—run amuck—jump—beat it!
farewell! fare-thee-well—good-bye! bye!
ah—bye-ye-ye!

We—of this earth—like this earth!
make heaven here—
take steps here—
to possess bearing hereafter—
dignity.

That we know how to enter:
reception room—drawing room—
banquet hall of:
abyssmal serious jester
whimsical serene power!
Poke ribs:
old son of gun—
old acquaintance!
Kiss: knees—toes!
Home—!
Our home!
We are home!
After:
smiling grim battle—
laughter—excitement—
swordplay—
sweat—
blood— —!
After accomplishing—
what sent for to accomplish.
Children of His loin—
Power of power.

Ferdinand Hardekopf

Ferdinand Hardekopf (1876–1954) was a little-known figure connected with Zurich Dada. A German poet who came to Dada after being associated with Expressionism, he participated in the soirees at the Cabaret Voltaire and in the group's other activities. A friend of Hans Richter and Albert Ehrenstein, he contributed to several issues of *Dada*.

Splendeurs et misères des débrouillards

Aus der steilen, transparenten Nudel
Quillt ein Quantum Quitten-Quark empor,
Ballt sich (physisch) zum gewürzten Strudel,
Kreist: ein Duft-Ballon aus einem Rohr.

Wann (und wo?) war Schweben delikater?
In der Spannung wird man blass, wie Chrom.
Lehr- und Schüler folgen dem Theater.
Doch der Stern geniesst sich autonom.

Hohe Hirnkraft wallt zu diesem Gase.
Da bestülpt der sachlichste Adept
Das Gestirn mit einem Stengelglase,
Darin dottrig etwas Ei verebbt.

Clear-Headed Splendors and Miseries

From the steep, transparent noodle
A quantity of quince curd quivers quietly,
Clings (physically) to the spicy strudel,
Circles: a fragrant balloon from a pipe.

When (and where?) was dangling more delicious?
The tension makes one as pale as chromium.
Teachers and pupils follow the theater.
Yet the star enjoys autonomy.

Great brain-power gravitates to this alley.
Here the most objective disciple inverts
The star with a wineglass,
In which some egg-yolk dies away.

Raoul Hausmann

Like his friend Johannes Baader, Raoul Hausmann (1886–1971) helped
determine the character of Berlin Dada and engaged in various icono-
clastic activities. A talented artist, writer, and photographer, the self-
proclaimed "Dadasoph" ("Dadasopher") founded *Der Dada* and coedited
Club Dada. However, he was best known as the inventor of photomon-
tage and the creator of optophonetic poetry. As he explained in *Courrier
Dada*, the latter art uses letters of different sizes to transcribe various
"respiratory and auditory combinations," much like musical notation.

bbbb . . .

bbbb
N' moum m'onoum onopouh
p
o
n
n
e
ee lousoo kilikilikoum
t' neksout coun' isoumt sonou
correyiosou out kolou
Y'IIITTITTTTIYYYH
kirriou korrothumn
N'onou
mousah
da
ou
DADDOU
irridadoumth
t' hmoum
kollokoum
o n o o o h h o o u u u m h n

kp' erioUM lp'er io u m

Nm' periii PERno-.-

bprEtiBerree eRREbEe e

ONNOo gplanpouk

konmpout PERIKOUL

nREEe e EEee rrrr..e.A

oapAerrre EEE

mgl ed padANou

MTNou tnou- t

Emmy Hennings

Emmy Hennings (1885–1948) was one of the key figures of Zurich Dada, together with her husband Hugo Ball. A talented actress, singer, and dancer, she was a cofounder of the Cabaret Voltaire where she often performed to Ball's piano accompaniment. In addition to participating in all the Dada activities, Hennings authored several novels and books of poetry and was involved with the reviews *Cabaret Voltaire* and *Dada*.

Gesang zur Dämmerung

Oktaven taumeln Echo nach durch graue Jahre.
Hochaufgetürmte Tage stürzen ein.
Dein will ich sein—
Im Grabe wachsen meine gelben Haare
Und in Hollunderbäumen leben fremde Völker
Ein blasser Vorhang raunt von einem Mord
Zwei Augen irren ruhelos durchs Zimmer
Gespenster gehen um beim Küchenbord.
Und kleine Tannen sind verstorbene Kinder
Uralte Eichen sind die Seelen müder Greise
Die flüstern die Geschichte des verfehlten Lebens.
Der Klintekongensee singt eine alte Weise.
Ich war nicht vor dem bösen Blick gefeit
Da krochen Neger aus der Wasserkanne,
Das bunte Bild im Märchenbuch, die rote Hanne
Hat einst verzaubert mich für alle Ewigkeit.

Morfin

Wir warten auf ein letztes Abenteuer
Was kümmert uns der Sonnenschein?
Hochaufgetürmte Tage stürzen ein
Unruhige Nächte—Gebet im Fegefeuer.

Wir lesen auch nicht mehr die Tagespost
Nur manchmal lächeln wir still in die Kissen.
Weil wir alles wissen, und gerissen
Fliegen wir hin und her im Fieberfrost.

Mögen Menschen eilen und streben
Heut fällt der Regen noch trüber
Wir treiben haltlos durchs Leben
Und schlafen, verwirrt, hinüber . . .

Twilight Song

Octaves stumble like echos through the gray years.
High-towered days crumble into ruins.
Yours will I be—
My blond hair grows in the grave
And a strange race lives in lilac trees
A pale curtain whispers about a murder
Two eyes wander restlessly through the room
Ghosts haunt the edge of the kitchen.
And little fir trees are dead children
Ancient oaks are the souls of tired old men
Who whisper the story of unsuccessful lives.
Lake Klintekongen sings an old tune.
I was not charmed before the evil glance
Negroes crawled from the water pitcher
The brightly colored picture in the book of fairytales, red Hanne
Once bewitched me for all eternity.

Morphine

We are waiting for one last adventure
What do we care about sunshine?
High-towered days crumble into ruins
Turbulent nights—prayer in Purgatory.

We no longer read the daily mail
Only sometimes do we smile quietly in the pillows,
Since we know everything, and fly
To and fro slyly in attacks of shivering.

Men may hurry and struggle
Today the rain still falls cheerlessly
We push unsteadily through life
And sleep, confused and exhausted . . .

Jacob van Hoddis

Jacob van Hoddis (1887–1942) was a friend of Hugo Ball and Emmy Hennings. Originally from Berlin, where he was active in Expressionist circles and where he published in *Der Sturm* and *Die Aktion*, he came to Zurich during the war. There he contributed to both *Cabaret Voltaire* and *Dada* and participated in the activities of the Zurich Dadaists.

Hymne

O Traum, Verdauung meiner Seele!
Elendes Combination womit ich vor Frost mich schütze
Zerstörer aller Dinge die mir Feind sind;
Aller Nachttöpfe,
Kochlöffel und Litfassäulen
O du mein Schiessgewehr!
In purpurne Finsternis tauchst du die Tage
Alle Nächte bekommen violette Horizonte
Meine Grossmama Pauline erscheint als Astralleib.
Und sogar ein Herr Sanitätsrat
Ein braver, aber etwas zu gebildeter
Sanitätsrat
Wird mir wieder amüsant
Er taucht auf aus seiner epheuumwobenen Ruhestätte
—War es nicht soeben ein himmelblauer Ofenschirm?
(He, Sie da!)
Und gackt: „Sogar — — —"
Frei nach Friedrich von Schiller.
O Traum, Verdauung meiner Seele
O du mein Schiessgewehr!
Gick! Gack!

Hymn

Oh dream, digestion of my soul!
Miserable scheme by which I protect myself against the frost
Destroyer of everything that threatens me;
Every chamber-pot,
Ladle, and advertising kiosque
Oh my firearm!
You immerse the days in crimson darkness
Every night acquires violet horizons
My Grandma Pauline appears as an astral body.
And even a member of the board of health
A worthy but womewhat over-educated
Member
Amuses me once more.
He emerges from his ivy-covered resting place
—Wasn't it just a sky-blue fireplace screen?
(Hey, you there!)
And cackles: "Even — — —"
Free after Friedrich von Schiller.
Oh dream, digestion of my soul
Oh my firearm!
Cluck! cluck!

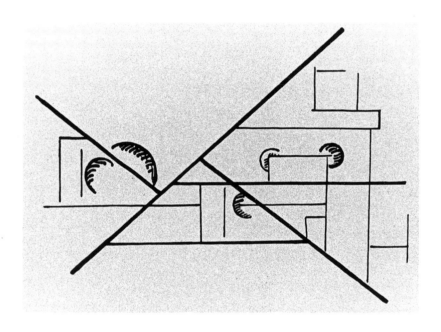

Theo van Doesburg, *The Mechanical Child*.

Richard Huelsenbeck

Richard Huelsenbeck (1892–1974) belonged to the initial Dada group at the Cabaret Voltaire in Zurich and took part in all their activities. In 1917 he settled in Berlin, where he cofounded another Dada group together with George Grosz, Raoul Hausmann, and John Heartfield. With Hausmann and Franz Jung he edited the journals *Club Dada* and *Der Dada* and lectured on Dada in Eastern Europe. In addition to publishing several volumes of poetry, he edited the *Dada Almanach* and wrote the first history of the movement: *En Avant Dada*.

391

Hans Arp gewidmet

Aus den Versenkungen steigen die jungen Hunde und schrein
wie die Kühe schreien sie mit ihren lakierten Mäulen
seht die Geheimräte mit den eingefallenen Bäuchen
Messingkübel haben sie über ihr Gesäss gestülpt, auf ihren
Händen hockt die junge Seekuh—eia, eia: es ist eine grosse Zeit
niemand weiss hinten wie er vorn daran ist
Haben Sie den Herrn gesehen der durch den Briefkasten steigt mit
    lächelndem Gesicht
Umba Umba sahen Sie die Kellerasseln mit gefalteten Händen
drei Tage schon geht die Prozession und immer noch flattert die Seele
    nicht
Ja ja Herr Doktor dies ist der Tag an dem ihre Grossmutter unter die
    Indianer ging
O - O - O
Der alte Kirchturm—der alte Mond Spinnwebmond Fliegenmond
ich halte die Hand auf den Bauch
der Schleiermond der grosse rote weite Mond
die Flüsse hinauf über die Berge gestemmt an die Sterne gereckt
jagen die jungen Hunde und schrein
es ist eine grosse Zeit

391

Dedicated to Hans Arp

The young hounds climb out of the hollows and bay
as the cows bawl with their lacquered muzzles
see the privy councilors with their emaciated bellies
They have crammed brass buckets on their butts, the young
Sea-cow squats on their hands, —eia, eia: it is a great time
thus no one behind knows what he is like in front
Have you seen the gentleman who climbs through the mailbox with a
         big smile
Umba umba did you see the cellar woodlice with pleated hands
the procession will leave in only three days and the soul is not yet
         restless
Yes yes Doctor this is the day when your grandmother joined the Indians
O - O - O
The old church-tower—the old moon spiderweb moon flying moon
I hold my hand on my belly
the veiled moon the great red moon
the rivers dammed up beyond the mountains stretching to the stars
the young hounds hunt and bay
it is a great time

Flüsse

Aus den gefleckten Tuben strömen die Flüsse in die Schatten der leben-
digen Bäume
Papageien und Aasgeier fallen von den Zweigen immer auf den Grund
Bastmatten sind die Wände des Himmels und aus den Wolken kommen
die grossen Fallschirme der Magier
Larven von Wolkenhaut haben sich die Türme vor die blendenden Augen
gebunden
O ihr Flüsse Unter der ponte dei sospiri fanget ihr auf Lungen und
Lebern und abgeschnittene Hälse
In der Hudsonbay aber flog die Sirene oder ein Vogel Greif oder ein
Menschenweibchen von neuestem Typus
mit eurer Hand greift ihr in die Taschen der Regierungsräte die voll sind
von Pensionen allerhand gutem Willen und schönen Leberwürsten
was haben wir alles getan vor euch wie haben wir alle gebetet vom
Skorpionstich schwillet der Hintern den heiligen Sängern und Ben
Abka der Hohepriester wälzt sich im Mist
eure Adern sind blau rot grün und orangefarben wie die Gesichte der
Ahnen die im Sonntagsanzuge am Bord der Altäre hocken
Zylinderhüte riesige o aus Zinn und Messing machen ein himmlisches
Konzert
die Gestalten der Engel schweben um eueren Ausgang als der Wider-
schein giftiger Blüten
so formet ihr euere Glieder über den Horizont hinaus in den Kaskaden
von seinem Schlafsofa stieg das indianische Meer die Ohren voll
Watte gesteckt
aus ihren Hütten kriechen die heissen Gewässer und schrein
Zelte haben sie gespannt von Morgen bis Abend über eurer Brunst und
Heere von Phonographen warten vor dem Gequäck eurer Lüste
ein Unglück ist geschehen in der Welt
die Brüste der Riesendame gingen in Flammen auf und ein Schlangen-
mensch gebar einen Rattenschwanz
Umba Umba die Neger purzeln aus den Hühnerställen und der Gischt
eueres Atems streift ihre Zehen
eine grosse Schlacht ging über euch hin und über den Schlaf eurer
Lippen
ein grosses Morden füllete euch aus

Rivers

The rivers pour from the speckled tubes into the shadows of the living
    trees
Parrots and vultures fall from the branches to the ground
The walls of the sky are fiber mats and the Magi's huge parachutes
    emerge from the clouds
The towers have fastened cloud-skin masks over their dazzling eyes
O you rivers Beneath the bridge of sighs you catch lungs and livers and
    slashed throats
But in Hudson Bay the siren flew or a condor or the newest type of hu-
    man female
Your hands reach into the pockets of the privy councilors which are full
    of all kinds of pensions good will and lovely liverwursts what we all
    did before you how we all prayed due to the scorpion sting the pos-
    teriors of the holy chorus are swelling and Ben Abka the high priest
    rolls in the manure
Your veins are blue red green and orange like the ancestors' faces who
    crouch on the altar's edge in their Sunday suits
Gigantic high silk hats o made of tin and brass create a heavenly concert
The shapes of angels hover around your exit as the reflection of poi-
    sonous flowers
Thus you form your limbs beyond the horizon in the cascades the Indian
    Ocean arose from its sofa bed its ears stuffed with cotton
The hot floods crawl from their huts and shriek
They have pitched tents from morning to evening over your passions
    and armies of phonographs wait before your quacking lust
a misfortune has befallen the world
the enormous lady's breasts went up in flames and a snake-man gave
    birth to a rat-tail
Umba umba the Negroes somersault out of the chicken coops and your
    breath's spray streaks their toes
a great battle passed over you and over your lips' sleep
a great slaughter filled you out

Matthew Josephson

Matthew Josephson (1899–1978), like Malcolm Cowley, was one of the Lost Generation who made their way to Paris after World War I. Sympathetic to the Dada spirit, he sought to spread the movement's message in two American expatriate reviews: *Secession* (published in Vienna) and *Broom* (published in Italy), which he coedited. As the title of his later book *Life Among the Surrealists* suggests, he was intimately associated with developments in Paris during the 1920s.

The Brain at the Wheel

To the man who knows
To the man who cares
To the man of taste
To the man of refinement
To the man with vision
To the man of the finer type and temperament of attire.

*   *   *

DO YOU FEAR THE DARK

As your Aboriginal Ancestors did? From their leafy dwellings in the primordial trees they peered ever anxiously into a profound darkness teeming with imaginary terrors.

But take the Lamp with the Clamp, clamp it on the mirror, clamp it on the table, clamp it on the bed, clamp it on the chair, or anywhere.

We bring
THE GIFT BEAUTIFUL
The Gift Supreme
What? What is to be?
Roses or worms? Or roses and worms?
Or is it seafood, snails, eels, mussels, clams and scallops?

*   *   *

With the brain at the wheel
the eye on the road
and the hand to the left
pleasant be your progress
explorer, producer, stoic, after your fashion.
Change
CHANGE
to what speed? to what underwear?
Here is a town, here a mill:
nothing surprises you old horse-face.
Guzzle-guzzle goes the siren;
and the world will learn to admire and applaud your concern about the
    parts, your firmness with employes, and your justice to your
    friends.
Your pride will not be overridden
Your faith will go unmortified.

Josep Maria Junoy

Josep Maria Junoy (1887–1955) was a poet, painter, and critic who was one of the principal animators of Barcelona Dada. Although he wrote in both Spanish and French, most of his compositions appeared in Catalan. In 1916 he founded the journal *Troços*, which became *Trossos* the following year when J. V. Foix became coeditor. Besides collaborating on numerous other reviews, such as *Proa* and *SIC*, Junoy published several collections of poetry and criticism. These include *Conferències de combat, 1919–1923* and *Poemes i cal·ligrames* (1920).

Eufòria

decisions sinòptiques

cos nu al sol

mentol al cor

una rosa color de rosa

espiral de rialles

Euphoria

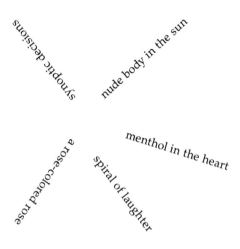

$C_2\,H_2$

botllofes pàl·lides
                 nues petites fades
       acetilenes
que
       sardanejen
       aquoses
a l'entorn del roc de carbur
  sota la llauna panteixanta
         prr . . .
          prr . . .
           prr . . .

            violetes

$C_2\,H_2$

pale blisters
            tiny naked acetylene
        fairies
who
        dance an aqueous
        sardana
around the pile of carbide
    beneath the gasping tin
            prr . . .
            prr . . .
            prr . . .

violets

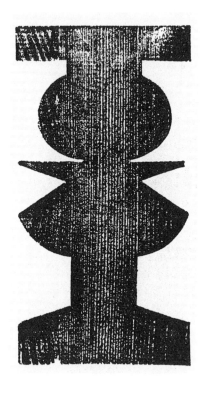

Hans (Jean) Arp, woodcut
(© Estate of Hans Arp / VAGA,
New York, 1991).

Rafael Lasso de la Vega

Rafael Lasso de la Vega (1890–1959) was a Spanish nobleman from Seville whose title was Marqués de la Villanova. Following a period of involvement with *modernismo*, he joined the Ultraist group in 1919, which was centered in Madrid. Soon thereafter he embraced Dada and became one of the principal proponents of the movement in Spain. The author of many books of poetry published in Spanish and French, Lasso contributed to numerous journals including *Grecia*, *Ultra*, and *Cosmópolis*.

Movimiento

He aqui la rueda asida a la ciudad
los dos regueros rojos que pasaron
se extinguen sucediéndose
                 y otros nuevos senderos
madeja circulante
pone en la manivela de sus nervios sutiles
los estampidos más gloriosos
equilibrios   timón de las audacias precavidas
              bajo sobre cerrado
pasan de un salto la flecha de los puentes
en circulos concéntricos
en divergencias que se escapan
y planos superpuestos
velozmente
              se ensanchan y se erigen
puntales de los cielos
torres que sostienen crepúsculos y auroras
manos tendidas hacia todos los puntos
sobre el mar y la tierra
              ansiedad desplegada
cada instante al pasar
la belleza cambia sus trajes infinitos
y el enigma dudoso cierra en cuatro dobleces

Movement

Here is the wheel attached to the town
the two red trails that passed
disappear behind each other
              and other new paths
circulating tuft
puts the most glorious explosions
in the crank of its subtle nerves
balances   rudder of the cautious audacities
              below above closed
they pass the bridges' arrow with a single leap
in concentric circles
in divergences that escape
and superimposed planes
rapidly
              there stretch out and are erected
pillars of the heavens
towers that support dusk and dawn
hands stretched in every direction
above the sea and on land
                  anxiety unfolded
each moment on passing
beauty changes its infinite costume
and the doubtful enigma closes in four folds

Conjunción abismo

La esquina solitaria otras veces
nadie habia visto atención clínica de urgencia
se necesitan aprendizas
la puertecilla de cristales de colores con luz dentro gira sola
y el farol rojo ante los anuncios pegados a la pared
En el gran silencio de mil orejas y en la soledad reducida
que mira estrechamente desde un millón de ojos
abierto toda la noche
se llama el paravant y es sabido
cosas misteriosas habrán pasado por aqui
horribles sombras, palabras en la obscuridad, pasos incertidumbres,
y tal vez nada a la luz de los reverberos de un diente
porque la noche se desploma desde los desvanes allá arriba
entre las chimeneas que se pasean en grupos
cogidas de las manos con sus sombreros de copa
llevan todas las llaves todas la campanillas todas las ventanas
y el viejo pequeño bar de la callejuela sonámbula
las fanfarrias de otras horas risueñas
y el siglo pasado
también los licores y las casas de vecindad y los music-halls
las puertas traseras de los teatros y el maquillage
todo de aqui a un momento no es prudente
lámpara discreta en el interior curiosidad
paraguas mojado señoras y señores bien entendido
a mano derecha, señorita mecanógrafa
peluquería, imprenta hace bastante frío
las piezas del ajedrez ahora
suena cló cló el canalon de diciembre
conversación ocurrencias el humo de la pipa
o el piano mecánico a estas horas con todas las revistas
y un bello rostro conocido hasta el día siguiente

Conjunction Abyss

The solitary corner other times
no one had seen attention emergency clinic
apprentices wanted
the little colored-glass door lit from within revolves alone
and the red lantern before the advertisements tacked to the wall
In the vast silence of a thousand ears and in the limited solitude
that watches closely from a million eyes
open all night
it is called a folding-screen and is well known
mysterious things must have happened around here
horrible shadows, words in the darkness, uncertain steps,
and perhaps nothing in the light of a tooth's reflections
because the night collapses from the attics up there
between the groups of chimneys that are taking a walk
hand in hand with their glass hats
they carry all the keys all the little bells all the windows
and the little old bar in the sonambulistic back street
the fanfares of other happy hours
and the previous century
also the liqueurs and the neighboring houses and the music halls
the stage entrances of the theaters and the makeup
everything here at one moment isn't prudent
discrete light bulb inside curiosity
dripping umbrella ladies and gentlemen of course
on the right hand, miss typist
barber shop, printing shop it's cold enough
the chess pieces now
the December drainpipe goes cluck cluck
conversation witticisms the pipe smoke
or the player piano at these times with all the magazines
and a beautiful face known until the next day

Diana

El hortera paseante en bicicleta sortilegio
compromiso con mi criada desnuda en el patio
Es la recepción perfumería en los alrededores del domingo
comadrona espiritual de las entidades periódicas
casa de dormir al servicio de la ley
soñando con la murga a pasos de entresuelo
sorbete y cine restaurant hebdomadario,
algarabía soleada de los bailables cartomancia

Diana

The shop assistant passing on his bicycle sorcery
a compromising situation with my naked maid on the patio
It is the reception perfumery in Sunday's outskirts
spiritual midwife of the periodical companies
hostel at the service of the law
dreaming with the street musicians to steps of mezzanine
sherbet and movies weekly restaurant
sun-dried arabic of the tea dances fortune telling

Signo

Alada y descendente
se oculta tras su nombre diáfano
linterna venturosa
apenas perceptible
lejos   roza la superficie de su voz
la alegria sin mancha
a la deriva
semáforos de todos los colores
señalan adióses sin destino

Transición

El avión de las mañanas
nos tendia su cuerda
Pero ahora las calles
cansadas de dar vueltas
desembocan en los baños del alba
Imágenes repletas de si mismas
se asoman hacia adentro
Las luces apagadas
El telón descorrido
Matices que enjuagan el silencio
Y todas estas cosas estaban aqui ya

Sign

Winged and descending
she hides behind her diaphanous name

lucky lantern
scarcely visible

far away   her voice's surface touches
flawless happiness

adrift
semaphores of every color
signal goodbye without destiny

Transition

Morning's airplane
offered us its cord

But now the streets
tired of going for walks
flow into the dawn's baths

Images crammed with themselves
take a brief look inside

The extinguished lights

The open curtain

Hues that rinse the silence

And all these things were already here

Halo

Todo
      inmóvil
se disgrega en palabras
ante mis ojos
      bello día
luz suavo y tranquila
          viviente
como el reloj de la consola
y mi sueño en la estancia
que separan cristales de la vida
exteriorizada en ruidos
          la calle
     va demasiado deprisa
Saldremos a lo que va y viene
      por escaleras que sucumben
a estos ríos
ce atolondradas galeras
     luces y atavíos
en una danza cotidiana
de brazos que me esperan
conversaciones y saludos
         Café
    El Sena y Notre-Dame
Literatura
    Antes de ayer

Halo

Everything
        immobile
disintegrates into words
before my eyes
        beautiful day
soft and tranquil light
          living
like the clock in the cabinet
and my dream in the room
which windows separate from life
represented by noises
        the street
    goes by too hurriedly
We will go out into the hustle and bustle
      by the stairs that succumb
to those rivers
of confused galleys
      lights and clothes
in a daily dance
of arms that promise me
conversations and greetings
         Cafe
    The Seine and Notre Dame
Literature
    The day before yesterday

Mina Loy

Mina Loy (1882–1966) was born in England and came to the United States after a period spent with the avant-garde in Paris and with the Italian Futurists. Married to the notorious Arthur Cravan, she figured prominently in New York Dada before moving to Paris in the early 1920s. An accomplished poet, playwright, and essayist, Loy acted with the Provincetown Players and published in journals such as *The Blind Man, Camera Work, Rogue, Others, The Little Review, Broom, Contact,* and *The Dial.*

Love Songs (excerpts)

I

Spawn of Fantasies
Sifting the appraisable
Pig Cupid   his rosy snout
Rooting erotic garbage
"Once upon a time"
Pulls a weed   white and star-topped
Among wild oats   sewn in mucous-membrane

I would   an   eye in a Bengal light
Eternity in a sky-rocket
Constellations in an ocean
Whose rivers run no fresher
Than a trickle of saliva

These   are suspect places

I must live in my lantern
Trimming subliminal flicker
Virginal   to the bellows
Of Experience
                  Coloured   glass

III

We might have coupled
in the bed-ridden monopoly of a moment
Or broken flesh with one another
At the profane communion table
Where wine is spill't on promiscuous lips

We might have given birth to a butterfly
With the daily-news
Printed in blood on its wings

V

Midnight empties the street
Of all but us
Three
I am undecided which way back
                To the left a boy
—One wing has been washed in the rain
   The other will never be clean any more—
Pulling door-bells to remind
Those that are snug
                To the right a haloed ascetic
                Threading houses
Probes wounds for souls
—The poor can't wash in hot water—
And I don't know which turning to take
Since you got home to yourself—first

Francesco Meriano

Francesco Meriano (1896–1934), who was associated with Italian Futurism for awhile, cofounded *La Brigata* in 1916 with Bino Binazzi. Living in Bologna, he corresponded with Tristan Tzara in Zurich and contributed poems to *Dada* and to the Roman review *Noi*. In addition, he authored a great many essays on various subjects, which appeared in assorted journals and which were collected in several volumes.

Walk

tirati in là Leopardi ti puzza il fiato estratto di pomodoro concentrato nel
vuoto
l'infinito esplode come un razzo di sagra metempsicosi dei fulmini e dei
ranocchi
colori tramontati
iride disincantata
sorriso putrefatto
aholaholaholahola
Cecco Becco muore tutte le sere
con goffe convulsioni umoristiche
Dada ultima rivista dell'universo
contiamoci quanti siamo
a voi buona sera Mr. Janco
a voi Mr. Tzara
uno
due
quattro
dieci
cinquanta
mille
veramente Marinetti parleremo alle stelle
dove le corazzate non scoppiano come trottole gigantesche
transalantico aeroceleste
l'infinito è nostro
Leopardi tirati in là ti puzzano i piedi.

Walk

dragged over there Leopardi your breath stinks tomato paste vacuum
    packed
infinity explodes like a festive rocket metempsychosis of lightning and
    frogs
faded colors
disenchanted iris
putrefied smile
aholaholaholahola
Uncle Carbuncle dies every night
with clumsy humorous convulsions
Dada ultimate review of the universe
let's count how many we are
good evening to you Mr. Janco
to you Mr. Tzara
one
two
four
ten
fifty
a thousand
truly Marinetti we will address the stars
where the battleships do not explode like gigantic tops
aero-celestial ocean liner
infinity is ours
Leopardi dragged over there your feet stink.

Hans (Jean) Arp, woodcut (© Estate of
Hans Arp / VAGA, New York, 1991).

Clément Pansaers

Although Clément Pansaers (1885–1922) belonged to the Belgian Dadaists, he participated in many of the activities in Paris. A member of the group centered around Francis Picabia, he contributed to the latter's review *391* and to *Littérature*, published by the future Surrealists. Determined to break with the past, like his character Zinzin, he was preoccupied above all with negation. Believing that Dada marked the beginning of a new era, he declared vehemently in *Littérature*: "Let the next generation worry about continuity!"

Ici finit la sentimentalité
(excerpt)

I

Je sonne
        je, cloche au pendentif de ma coupole.
Le gars berce son ours:—roulis et tangage—mouvement quadruple
autour des quatre dimensions de la verticale.
Ouverts les accumulateurs—la station d'énergie dépasse la supériorité,
        —l'ours berce le gars—
                    traverse
les degrés de la progression arithmétique, la raison, et géométrique,—
fluide . . . anti—a-négatif, a-positif, a-neutre—où le quotient se trans-
forme:
le brut et l'organisé s'entre-pénètrent; le stable équilibre vacille;—le vice
et la vertu, entre-pétrifiés, filent en deux nuances ultra-, infra-, enfilés;—
le moral, l'immoral, l'amoral: l'absurde et le logique, inclivables, en sym-
étrie asymétrique, kaléidoscopique, en temps, espace—
—Gars et ours se bercent en une station d'énergie centrale—
A l'intersection du perceptible et de l'imperceptible: le cheveu du gars,
merveille blonde, saisit le poil de l'ours.
Au mouvement de l'écartelage de l'acte en quatre dimensions, la ver-
ticale vibre A: un tourbillon syncopant sonore A . . .
Ours et gars se berçant au tremplin du vide: cube, cône, sphère, tour-
billonnent dans l'inertie:—les cristaux atomiques poreux s'anéantissent
et . . .
        le rien chaotique éclate.
Se volatilisent diatoniques entre le bruit et le silence, les vocalises A . . .
Du gars, au désir d'élever son ours de la zone insensible à la sensible—le
sensible se sentimentalise;
dans le ventre de l'ours, le grelot sonne du jouet la sentimentalité enfan-
tine.
Je, cloche, du pendentif de ma coupole dégringole:
                        les tessons sur la
pierre répercutent les éclats en A . . .

Sentimentality Stops Here
(excerpt)

I

I ring out
      I, a bell in my dome's pendentive.
The lad cradles his bear: — rolling and pitching — quadruple movement
about the vertical's four dimensions.
Batteries switched on — the power station exceeds mere superiority,
         — the bear cradles the lad —
                           climbs
the steps of the geometrical and, reason, arithmetical progression — anti-
fluid . . . —a-negative, a-positive, a-neutral — where the quotient is
transformed:
crudity and organization interpenetrate; the stable equilibrium wavers —
interpetrified, vice and virtue flow threaded together in two ultra-,
infra-nuances — morality, immorality, amorality: absurdity and logic
welded together in kaleidoscopic, asymmetrical symmetry, in time,
space —
Lad and bear cradle each other in a power station — At the intersection of
the perceptible and the imperceptible: one of the lad's marvelously blond
hairs clings to the bear's fur.
At the moment the act is quartered into four dimensions, the vertical
vibrates in A: a syncopated sonorous whirlwind in A . . .
Bear and lad cradling each other on the void's trampoline: cube, cone,
sphere whirl in the inertia: — the porous atomic crystals annihilate each
other and . . .
               chaotic nothingness bursts forth.
The vocal exercises in A evaporate in the diatonic intervals between the
noise and the silence . . . Wishing to raise his bear from an insensible to
a sensible state — the lad's sensibility yields to sentiment; in the bear's
belly, the toy bell sounds a note of childish sentimentality.
I, a bell, tumble from my dome's pendentive:
                             the broken pieces on the
stone floor echo the fragments in A . . .

Joan Pérez-Jorba

Joan Pérez-Jorba (1878–1928) was one of the principal literary and artistic links between France and Catalonia. Situated in Paris where he edited a journal called *L'Instant* ("*Revue Franco-Catalane d'art et littérature*"), he published several books of poetry and criticism. Equally at home in French or Catalan, Pérez contributed to numerous reviews in both languages. Besides *Dada* these included *La Revue de l'Epoque*, *SIC*, *Messidor*, *Plançons*, *El Cami*, and *Noi*.

Elle a deux têtes

Il voulut s'agenouiller

                        les autos cornaient essouflés

devant les blessures les flammes sanglantes

                               que la lumière ouvrait

                               à travers les portes

le clown devint alors livide impavide

dans sa soie

                  il regardait tout déçu

                  filer par le couloir sans mot diré

dans la rue

un faune courait aussi vers le tramway électrique

qui courait lui aussi à toute allure dans la mer

             il lui prit une envie

                  de rire et de maudire

mais il lui semblait que la lumière voulait lui parler

                      de ce dont il n'avait jamais ouï dire

comme il tremblait

il posa ses mains sur ses tempes

               il bafoua la beauté antique

               il perdit connaissance

dans les espaces emmurés tout autour

            sous les yeux bleus du jour

She Has Two Heads

He wanted to kneel
                              the cars honked breathlessly
before the wounds the bloody flames
                                    that the light opened
                                    through the doors
then the clown became livid intrepid
in his silk
                              he watched with great disappointment
                              leaving by the hallway silently
in the street
a faun also ran toward the electric streetcar
which also was running at full speed into the sea
                    He felt like
                              laughing and cursing
but it seemed the light wanted to speak to him
                    about something he had never heard of
as he was trembling
he put his hands on his temples
                              he jeered at ancient beauty
                              he lost consciousness
in the spaces enclosed by walls
              beneath the daylight's blue eyes

Comme un chien

Elle court comme un chien après son rêve
marchand d'habits! là dans la cour
       où le linge sale s'étale
le tramway court entre les arbres qui dansent
           sans trêve ni sève
la cloche tinte dans mes oreilles et dans mon coeur
      qui donc a soufflé sur la bougie de mon amour?
penses-y sans douleur mon coeur
elle est pâle

Arpège

De la lumière avec les dreadnoughts à ses trousses
           des roses sans chemise
une larme une seule
            l'aéroplane d'un paillasse
un joli rire d'enfant
        sur la mansarde
des rayons des ailerons
       ton ame
un chant mélodieux
      comme des yeux
         et bizarre

Like a Dog

She runs like a dog after her dream
clothes merchant! there in the courtyard
        where the dirty linen is hanging
the streetcar runs between the trees that dance
                without truce or juice
the bell tinkles in my ears and in my heart
    who has blown out the candle of my love?
think about it painlessly my heart
she is pale

Arpeggio

Some light with the dreadnoughts on its heels
                some shirtless roses
a tear only one
                a clown's airplane
a child's laugh
            on the mansard roof
rays pinions
        your soul
a melodious song
        like eyes
                and bizarre

Bouffées de fumée

.

Il pense à des riens et n'écoute plus
                              dans sa Tête
le bruit des usines fait un roulement de tambour
son cou se penche doucement sur son réve
                                      mais
la joie inespérée du mensonge d'amour entre en lui
        On marche dans l'appartement du dessous
        c'est comme un remous
Sur un case ébréché l'âme violente du poète
            il fait un paquet de ses idées
            et s'en va vers la Seine
            jeter les bouffées de fumée de son cigare

Puffs of Smoke

He is thinking of trifles and is not listening
                                    in his Head
the factory noise makes a drumroll
his neck bends softly over his dream
                        but
the unexpected joy of love's falsehood enters him
          Someone is walking in the lower apartment
          it's like an eddy
The poet's violent soul on a chipped vase
               he wraps up his ideas
               and goes off toward the Seine
               to discard puffs of his cigar smoke

Francis Picabia

Francis Picabia (1879–1953) was one of the key figures in the international Dada movement. During World War I and afterwards, he participated in Dada activities in New York, Barcelona, Zurich, and Paris. A multi-talented individual, he published several books of poetry, painted continuously, and edited a series of Dada journals. The most important of these was *391*, but the list also includes *Cannibale*, *Le Pilhaou-Thibaou*, and *La Pomme de pins*. His ballet *Relâche* and his scenario for the film *Entr'acte* (both 1924) brought the Dada period to a close with a resounding finale.

Tambourin

Les habitudes ont l'oeil rusé
Comme les mailles d'un filet
l'ivrogne va de village en village
Cherchant des amis
les mouches voltigent avant de mourir
Comme des petits projectiles
La musique passe dans la rue
Notre oreille la suit
Il faut aller jusqu'au bout du monde
Mais le bout du monde est décoloré par le soleil

L'Oeil froid

Après notre mort, on devrait nous mettre dans une boule, cette boule serait en bois de plusieurs couleurs. On la roulerait pour nous conduire au cimetière et les croque-morts chargés de ce soin, porteraient des gants transparents, afin de rappeler aux amants le souvenir des caresses.

Pour ceux qui désireraient enrichir leur ameublement du plaisir objectif de l'être cher, il existerait des boules en cristal, au travers desquelles on apercevrait la nudité définitive de son grand-père ou de son frère jumeau!

Sillage de l'intelligence, lampe steeple-chase ; les humains ressemblent aux corbeaux à l'oeil fixe, qui prennent leur essor au-dessus des cadavres—et tous les peaux-rouges sont chefs de gare!

Tambourine

Habits have a crafty eye
Like the mesh of a net
the drunkard goes from village to village
Searching for friends
the flies flit to and fro before dying
Like tiny projectiles
Our ears follow the music
As it passes by in the street
One should go to the ends of the world
But the world's ends are faded from the sun.

The Cold Eye

After our death we should be put into a ball. This ball would be made of different colored woods. They would roll us to the cemetery, and the undertakers charged with this duty would wear transparent gloves in order to remind the lovers of past caresses.

For those who would like to enrich their furnishings with the objective pleasure of the loved one, there would exist balls made of crystal through which one would perceive the definitive nudity of one's grandfather or twin brother!

Wake of the intelligence, lamp steeplechase; human beings resemble crows with fixed eyes which take to the air above the corpses, and all the redskins are stationmasters!

L'Enfant

L'automne est fané,
par l'enfant
que nous aimons.
Ainsi qu'un vautour
sur une charogne,
il diminue sa famille
puis disparait
comme un papillon . . .

Tous les jours

La nuit brille comme des feuilles de verre
J'ai compris
Les feuilles se couvrent de nuages
Nouvelle aventure
La nuit toute neuve
Qui se balance en l'air comme une béquille
Infirme
Dans la maison je suis sur une petite échelle.

The Child

Autumn is tarnished
by the child
whom we love.
Like a vulture
upon carrion
he diminishes his family
then disappears
like a butterfly . . .

Everyday

The night glistens like leaves of glass
I have understood
The leaves cover themselves with clouds
New adventure
The brand new night
Which balances in the air like a shaky
Crutch
In the house I am on a stepladder.

Bonheur

Je veux que l'objet
Comme l'alcool païen
Gribouille l'estomac de la raison
Et que le chant du coq

Maudisse le soleil
Passe-temps du diable
Lubies quel bonheur
Je me porte bien
Au hasard.

Fleur coupée

Nous habitions le même âge
dans une ville déserte
et le rideau électrique
introduisait deux fois ses batteries
dans une boite d'allumettes bizarres

Francis Picabia 161

Happiness

I want objects
Like pagan alcohol
To scrawl the stomach of reason
And the cock's crow
To curse the sun
The devil's pastime
Whims what happiness
I proceed entirely
At random.

Cut Flower

We inhabited the same age
in a deserted city
and the electric curtain
twice inserted its batteries
into a box of bizarre matches

Cacodylate

Sa parade dont l'ébullition a des bornes impitoyables
faisait cortège d'un oeil cacodylate rose vif
dans ma vie de suralimentation suisse.
Les chaises longues existaient après la mort
ce qu'elles pensaient couvre l'abandon c'est net
tout cela dans un peu de cristal médecin—

Je m'en fais gloire infiniment des bibelots d'ivoire
dussé-je souffrir aujourd'hui pendant ce long trajet
vers le peignoir rose en plis de cierges allumés—

Abominablement la science comme un dépôt
limite le coeur avec une invisible caresse
dans je ne sais quoi, mais en rond—

Les livres spirales caractérisent d'intimes délicatesses
de petit Saxe gisant épars partout où se glisse
la passagère flottante d'isolement chocolat.

Elle m'a laissé sa main d'hygiène arsenic
à cette place meurtrie d'accalmie froncée
comme le foyer d'un nouveau lit nuptial.

Cacodylate

Her parade whose effervescence has pitiless boundaries
proceeded with a bright pink cacodylate eye
in my life of Swiss overfeeding.
The lounging chairs existed after death
what they thought covers the neglect that's clear
all that in a bit of doctor crystal—

I glory infinitely in the ivory trinkets
should I have to suffer today during this long journey
toward the pink dressing gown in pleats of lighted tapers—

Abominably science like a warehouse
restricts the heart with an invisible caress
in I don't know what, but circular—

The spiral books represent intimate frailties
of bits of Dresden china scattered everywhere she glides
the floating passenger of chocolate isolation.

She has left me her hand of arsenic hygiene
in this bruised place of frowning calm
like the entrance to a new marriage bed.

Raoul Hausmann, linocut (© Raoul
Hausmann / VAGA, New York, 1991).

Giuseppe Raimondi

Giuseppe Raimondi (1898–) was the editor of *La Raccolta*, an eclectic journal published in Bologna. In addition to occupying himself with the diffusion of Dada in Italy, he was in touch with the Zurich group and contributed a poem to *Dada*. Other poems appeared in *Avanscoperta* and *La Brigata*. Raimondi was also the author of numerous essays and several volumes of criticism.

Resurrezione

Magìa degli antichi arcobaleni lunari
 Sconsacrata giovinezza
 da quando le primavere eroiche finirono nelle composizioni
  tipografiche
Non c'è più la città incandescente che sale dalle 4 croci nell'azzurro sonoro
 dietro il ponte
I ricordi sono appesi alle finestre della nostra via di smalto
I notturni dialoghi
 colle divinità astrali
Poichè la nostra vita
 la trovi nel miracolo cabalistico lagoro lagurai
             mü balli
Labbra verdi al sole delle armonie stellari
La giovinezza l'abbiam lasciata per mancia in un albergo artico
A tutti gli angoli dell'universo c'è il promesso Nirvana
Fanfare di esclamazioni per la fanciullezza dei popoli
I canti dei negri!
Esplosione in piani di luce
I colpi di tamburo dell'aurora abbattono i cieli

Resurrection

Magic of the ancient lunar rainbows
    Desecrated youth
    from when the heroic springtimes ended in typographical compositions
No longer is it the incandescent city that emerges from the 4 crosses
    in the resonant azure beyond the bridge
Memories are hung out the windows of our enameled life
Noctural dialogues
    with the astral divinities
Since you find our life
    in the cabalistic miracle   lagoro lagurai
                      mü balls
Green lips in the stellar harmonies' sun
We left our youth as a present in an arctic inn
At every corner of the universe the promised Nirvana appears
Fanfares of cries by the populace's childhood
Negro songs!
Explosion in planes of light
The dawn's drumbeats destroy the heavens

Man Ray

Man Ray (1890–1976) was a quintessential Dada spirit. Primarily a painter and photographer, he was an important member of New York Dada, frequenting the Arensberg circle in particular. Among other things, he edited a journal called *The Ridgefield Gazook* and later coedited *New York Dada* with his friend Marcel Duchamp. He also collaborated with Duchamp on photographic objects and collages, including the film *Anemic Cinema*. In 1921 Ray moved to Paris and became an active member of the Dada group there.

L'Inquiétude

1 '' 23456789 10 11 12 : : : : : : : -ITTTTTI- Qh

Dragnnnnnnnnnnnnnnnnnn

(Petite)   *|Droooooooooooooo.

PI!TY

I'll see you again soon, yes, sooon.

Thought : (sooner than you think) soune or suun !

Collender 1920

Wetch by time

1 2 3 4 5 6 7 8 9 10 11 12 S M T W T F S

Georges Ribemont-Dessaignes

Georges Ribemont-Dessaignes (1884–1974) was an active member of
Paris Dada and collaborated on several projects with Francis Picabia.
The author of numerous poems and four or five Dada plays, including
L'Empereur de Chine and *Le Serin muet*, he published some ten novels and
volumes of essays. His mechanomorphic drawings and paintings ap-
peared in a wide range of publications, from *Cannibale, 391*, and *Littéra-
ture* to journals such as *De Stijl, Mecano*, and *Die Schammade*.

Trombone à coulisse

J'ai sur la tête une petite ailette qui tourne au vent
Et me monte l'eau à la bouche
Et dans les yeux
Pour les appétits et les extases
J'ai dans les oreilles un petit cornet plein d'odeur d'absinthe
Et sur le nez un perroquet vert qui bat des ailes
Et crie : Aux Armes!
Quand il tombe du ciel des graines de soleil
L'absence d'acier au coeur
Au fond des vieilles réalités débossées et croupissantes
Est partiale aux marées lunatiques
Je suis capitaine et alsacienne au cinéma
J'ai dans le ventre une petite machine agricole
Qui fauche et lie des fils électriques
Les noix de coco que jette le singe mélancolie
Tombent comme crachats dans l'eau
Ou refleurissent en pétunias
J'ai dans l'estomac une ocarina et j'ai le foie virginal
Je nourris mon poète avec les pieds d'une pianiste
Dont les dents sont paires et impaires
Et le soir des tristes dimanches
Aux tourterelles qui rient comme l'enfer
Je jette des rêves morganatiques

Slide Trombone

I have a small propeller on my head that turns in the wind
And draws water up into my mouth
And into my eyes
For various appetites and ecstasies
I have a little horn in my ears which is full of the smell of absinthe
And on my nose a green parrot who flaps his wings
And cries "To Arms!"
When seeds of sunlight fall from the sky
The absence of steel in my heart
At the bottom of ancient stagnating and level realities
Is partial to the lunatic tides
I am a captain and an Alsatian at the cinema
I have a little agricultural machine in my belly
Which reaps and binds electric wires
The coconuts that monkey melancholy throws
Fall like spit in the water
Or flourish anew as petunias
I have an ocarina in my stomach and I have a virginal liver
I nourish my poet with a pianist's feet
Whose teeth are even and uneven in number
And at night on sad Sundays
I throw Morganatic dreams
To the turtledoves who laugh like hell

Elle a les seins . . .

Elle a les seins terminés par une plume d'oie qui scarifie les
cheveux poèmes des rues closes
Tant de petits chapeaux qui couvrent les frontières du beurre durci
S'agitent comme des tambours
Se sucent comme des dragées
Et son sourire perpétue sur un fil sans fil les oreilles obcènes ou
meurt sa salive
Les ouvertures de son ventre ont une utilité qu'on voit sur son nez
Maris il pleut si fort des chemins de fer chauffés avec des nids
d'oasis
Qu'on peut bien prendre des bains de pieds de mélancolie sans
mouiller les bas de soie des collections de coeur
Qu'elle enroule autour de son cou
Comme le Jardin des Plantes
Petits espoirs chimiques sous les ongles sales ont été mangés comme
des amants
Que reste-t-il a faire de cette putain morte qui chemine autour de
la rate cuisinière
Elle crache en l'air de si beaux petits pigeons
Et chante si bien mon nom
Je dirai partout que je suis ministre et balayeur
Mais dans les coins obscurs je ferai l'amour avec ses cils

Each of Her Breasts . . .

Each of her breasts ends in a goose feather which scarifies her
hair poems of the closed streets
So many little hats that cover the edges of the hardened butter
Become agitated like drums
Suck on themselves like Jordan almonds
And her smile perpetuates on a wireless wire the obscene ears in
which her saliva dies
The openings in her belly have a use that one sees on her nose
But it is raining trains heated with oasis nests so hard
That you can take feet of melancholy baths without
Wetting your silk stockings from the heart collections
That she wraps around her neck
Like the Arboretum
Small chemical hopes beneath the dirty fingernails have been eaten
like lovers
What remains to be done with this dead whore who travels around
the kitchen pulse
She spits such pretty little pigeons into the air
And sings my name so well
I will tell everyone that I am a minister and a sweeper
But in the obscure corners I will make love to her lashes

Joan Salvat-Papasseit

Joan Salvat-Papasseit (1894–1924) has come to be regarded as one of the two best poets writing in Catalan—and occasionally Spanish—during the early twentieth century. (The other is J. V. Foix.) Although his poetry reveals considerable Futurist influence, some of the poems reflect the Dada spirit by virtue of their vehement dislocation. During his brief life, Salvat published no fewer than five volumes of poetry and edited four separate reviews: *Un Enemic del Poble, Arc Voltaic, Mar Vella,* and *Proa.*

Historia sin interés

el reloj cadmio de la Bolsa ha quedado disuelto en el frio del aire y en la lluvia plateada serpentina

dentro de la fachada los contables lunáticos han tanteado el suelo

(se han perdido 3 horas de la esfera y los orondos dólares han subido 3 veces la tarima castrada por los ceros)

el hombre del sombrero de 2 picos ha escondido un minuto en su *serviette* negra y ha gritado después:

—LO HACEMOS
MOVER TODO   LO HACEMOS
LO HACEMOS   MOVER TODO
MOVER TODO

el minuto robado ha vuelto a aparecer y ha empezado la rumba de los millones ebrios

la multitud de *stylos* y de lápices-tinta han librado batalla: LO HACEMOS MOVER TODO

YO ENTRO CON MI "HORSE POWER" EN LA BOLSA

A Story of No Interest

the Stock Exchange's cadmium clock is still dissolved in the cold air and in the silver-plated serpentine rain

behind the facade the lunatic accountants have estimated how the land lies

(its face has lost
3 hours and the potbellied dollars have thrice ascended the platform castrated by the zeros)

the man in the two-cornered hat hid a minute in his black napkin and then cried:

—WE MAKE IT ALL
WORK   WE MAKE IT
WE MAKE IT ALL   ALL WORK
WORK

the stolen minute has appeared again and the rumba of the drunken millions has begun

the multitude of ballpoint pens and ink pencils have engaged in battle:
WE MAKE IT ALL WORK

I ENTER THE STOCK EXCHANGE WITH MY "HORSE POWER"

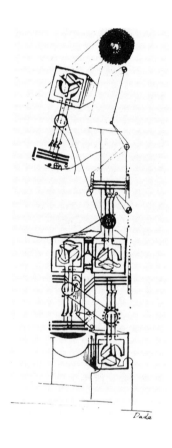

Max Ernst, *Dada* (COPYRIGHT 1992
ARS, N.Y. / SPADEM / ADAGP).

Bino San Miniatelli

Bino San Miniatelli (1896–) was a prolific poet, novelist, and short story writer who founded the review *Noi* together with Enrico Prampolini. Of mixed Dada and Futurist tendencies, the latter journal—published in Rome—featured numerous contributions by the Zurich group. In return Miniatelli's name appeared in *Dada* from time to time where he published the poem "Concime."

Concime

Manti vitali
di putride sonnolenze.
Svolazzare a spirali—terra terra—
come farfalloni che si disfanno.
Sacrifici d'insetti.
Armonia cronometrica
della decomposizione.
Bollore d'accoppiamenti profondi
come un ronzar febbrile di falene.
Le lune piene—le lune galleggianti
sull' erbe scapigliate—
come pallon volanti
su su pel cielo sono montate—
vuote—senza splendore—
aspergendo di sterile albore
il talamo fremente—di concime bollente.
Il porco ha grugnito
rufolando nel mucchio del concio
come un torvo re preistorico—
un Turno re de' Rutoli—il grugno fitto
nel concio—parlare incomprensibile
scuotendo la brutale—testa sulle male
sorti d'un esercito sconfitto.
E le farfalle si sono spogliate
dell ali leggendarie—variopinte
nell' aureola de' cieli profondi—
si sono sfarfallate.
La vigna nell' ombria
de' suoi peccati in fiore—
sotto a un fumante tumulo
di concio—vigile stallone—

Manure

Vital cloaks
of putrid somnolence.
Flying around in spirals—near the ground—
like large butterflies demolishing themselves.
Insect sacrifices.
Chronometric harmony
of decomposition.
Excitement of intense couplings
like a feverish whirring of moths.
Full moons—moons floating
above the rumpled grass—
like flying balloons
they have climbed up up in the sky—
empty yourselves—without splendor—
sprinkling the quivering nuptial bed
with sterile brightness—
with boiling manure.
The hog grunted
rooting in the pile of manure
like a hideous prehistoric king—
a Turnus king of Rutoli—his snout stuck
in the manure—incomprehensible speech
shaking his brutal head over the bad
luck of a defeated army.
And the butterflies stripped themselves
of their legendary wings—variegated
in the heavens' haloed depths—
they de-butterflied themselves.
The vine in the shadow
of its flowering sins—
beneath a reeking tomb
of manure—wary stallion—

fiduciosa s'è sdraiata —
d' essere fecondata.
Una gallina fradicia — che maturava al sole —
stechita e macolata —
ha fatto coccodè
perchè il bambino — che ci si divertiva
sull' ala — come con un burattino —
per finire la festa
le ha messo un piede sulla testa.
Tutti gli insetti hanno suonato i campanelli
alla baldoria — alla baldoria
di Re Concime — vulcano leggendario —
rinvigorire tic tac — i sonni contadini.
Ma la notte era cosi stellata
(o! quella notte stellata
com' era matematica . . .) che un nero
scarabeo passeggero
si credeva uno specchio.

lay down trustingly —
to be fertilized.
A rotten hen — that was ripening in the sun —
stiff and bruised —
began to cluck
because the boy — who was amusing himself
on the threshing floor — as with a puppet —
put one foot on its head
to finish the festival.
All the insects sounded the bells
at the feast — at the feast of King Manure — legendary volcano —
to invigorate tic toc — the peasant slumbers.
But the night was so starry
(oh! that starry night
how mathematical it was . . .) that a black
scarab passing by
mistook itself for a mirror.

Kurt Schwitters

Kurt Schwitters (1887–1948) was a German artist and writer situated in Hanover. Known especially for his junk collages, he was also a practicing poet who experimented with sound poetry (*Ursonate*) and other advanced forms. He used the term *merz*—borrowed from the label *Kommerzbank* in one of his collages—to describe his compositions. An important conduit for Holland Dada, Schwitters edited a review entitled *Merz* from 1923 to 1932 and collaborated on reviews such as *Mecano* and *Der Zeltweg*.

Gedicht No. 48

Wanken.
Regenwurm.
Fische.
Uhren.
Die Kuh.
Der Wald blättert die Blätter.
Ein Tropfen Asphalt in den Schnee.
Cry, cry, cry, cry, cry.
Ein weiser Mann platzt ohne Gage.

Es ist Herbst

Es ist Herbst. Die Schwäne essen das Brot ihrer Herren mit
Tränen zusammengebacken. Einige matte Expressionisten
schreien nach Wein, denn es ist noch Wein genug da, aber es
gibt keinen Expressionismus mehr.
Es lebe der Kaiser, denn es gibt keinen Kaiser mehr. Uhren
uhren die Stunden fünfundzwanzigtausendmal.
Ich gleite.
Gleite Schlingen.
Kreischt eine Maschine.
Katzen hängen an der Wand.
Ein Jude geigt das Tier zum Fenster hinaus.
Heraus.
Es ist Herbst und die Schwäne herbsten auch.

Poem No. 48

Stagger.
Earthworm.
Fishes.
Clocks.
The cow.
The forest leafs the leaves.
A drop of asphalt in the snow.
Cry, cry, cry, cry, cry,
A wise man explodes without a salary.

It Is Autumn

It is autumn. The swans eat their masters' bread
baked with tears. A few feeble Expressionists
cry for wine, since there is still enough wine, but
there is no more Expressionism.
Long live the Kaiser, since there is no more Kaiser. Clocks
clock the hours twenty-five thousand times.
I am sliding.
Sliding Snares.
A machine screams.
Cats hang on the wall.
A Jew fiddles the animal out the window.
Out.
It is autumn, and the swans autumnize also.

An Anna Blume

Oh Du, Geliebte meiner 27 Sinne, ich liebe Dir!
Du, Deiner, Dich Dir, ich Dir, Du mir, — — — —wir?
Das gehört beiläufig nicht hierher!

Wer bist Du, ungezähltes Frauenzimmer, Du bist, bist Du?
Die Leute sagen, Du wärest.
Laß sie sagen, sie wissen nicht, wie der Kirchturm steht.

Du trägst den Hut auf Deinen Füßen und wanderst auf die Hände,
Auf den Händen wanderst Du.

Halloh, Deine roten Kleider, in weiße Falten zersägt,
Rot liebe ich Anna Blume, rot liebe ich Dir.
Du, Deiner, Dich Dir, ich Dir, Du mir, — — — — —wir?
Das gehört beiläufig in die kalte Glut!
Anna Blume, rote Anna Blume, wie sagen die Leute?

   Preisfrage:

      1.) Anna Blume hat ein Vogel,
      2.) Anna Blume ist rot.
      3.) Welche Farbe hat der Vogel.

Blau ist die Farbe Deines gelben Haares,
Rot ist die Farbe Deines grünen Vogels.
Du schlichtes Mädchen im Alltagskleid,
Du liebes grünes Tier, ich liebe Dir!
Du Deiner Dich Dir, ich Dir, Du mir, — — — —wir!
Das gehört beiläufig in die— — —Glutenkiste.

To Anna Blume

Oh you, beloved of my 27 senses, I love your!
You, yours, you, your, I your, your mine. —we?
Incidentally this belongs somewhere else!

Who are you, uncounted lady, you are, are you?
People say, you might be.
Let them talk, they don't know how the church tower stands.

You wear your hat on your feet and wander on your hands,
On your hands you wander.

Hello, your red dress, cut up into white pleats,
Red I love Anna Blume, red I love your.
You, yours, you, your, I your, you mine. —we?
Incidentally this belongs in the chilly heat!
Anna Blume, red Anna Blume, what do people say?

> *Prize Question:*
>
> 1) Anna Blume has a bird,
> 2) Anna Blume is red.
> 3) What color is the bird.

Blue is the color of your yellow hair,
Red is the color of your green Bird.
You simple maiden in ordinary dress,
You dear green animal, I love your!
You, yours, you, your, I your, you mine. —we!
Incidentally this belongs in the—heatbox.

Anna Blume, Anna, A— — — —N— — — —N— — — —A!
Ich träufle Deinen Namen.
Dein Name tropft wie weiches Rindertalg.
Weißt Du es Anna, weißt Du es schon,
Man kann Dich auch von hinten lesen.
Und Du, Du Herrlichste von allen,
Du bist von hinten, wie von vorne:
A— — — — — —N— — — — — —N— — — — — —A.
Rindertalg träufelt STREICHELN über meinen Rücken.
Anna Blume,
Du tropfes Tier,
Ich— — — — — — —liebe— — — — — — —Dir!

Anna Blume, Anna, A—N—N—A!
I let your name fall in drops.
Your name drips like soft tallow.
Do you know it, do you already know it,
One can also read you from behind.
And you, you the most magnificent of all,
You are the same from behind as from before:
A— — — — — —N— — — — — —N— — — — — —A.
Tallow drops CARESSINGLY on my back.
Anna Blume,
You dripping animal,
I— — — — — — —love— — — — — — —your!

Walter Serner

Walter Serner (1889–ca. 1942) was an Austrian physician who founded a journal called *Sirius* in Zurich in 1915. In addition to participating in Zurich Dada activities, he contributed to *Dada* and coedited *Der Zeltweg* with Tristan Tzara and Otto Flake. Among his diverse contributions, he published poems in several reviews, authored a manifesto entitled *Letzte Lockerung*, and helped organize a Dada ball in Geneva.

Bestes Pflaster auch roter Segen

Bodenbepurzelndes Geschirr:
gar so süss soffen Ninallas Lippen Pommery greno first.
Minkoff, ein ganz ein Russischer, déroutiert nebengeleisig.
Vorüberflappernder Handteller: benützter Busen bläht Blondes.
Pauschal.   Schal.
Schluck Wein (Länge: 63 centimètres) in rotverbesserte Nüstern
gespien.   Queen!!!
Weil ensembletapfer beflüstert Kuno feistes Postérieur.
Knäuel, dem sich schweissig Unterarm entzupft.
Vornübergewettert: Sibi schrie naturgemäss immens auf,
Hemigloben nach oben.
Derzeit brennendes Pedal berutscht entzückt anderwärts gestreichelten
Bauch.   Auch.
Unüberholt wischt seine lingua fettesten Schenkel einher, Isidor.
O wie lieb ich das Gelichter des Lebens! (Abends, naturellement!)
Kruschewaz glotzt auf die ach so entfernten Deltafalten Zuzzis.
Baynes Destiny (Massachusetts-allerholdest) quillt geigengeil um die Ecke;
Blech taumelt daraus schwierig empor:
schwachbeflorter Unterleib (?Gaby!) wogt taktvoll heran.
"Die Treue ist kein hohler Zahn" . . . (Kreuzung von Kind und Kegel)
Madame V. flicht, sehr gewiegt, Roger ein Glas in die Finger;
quetscht das Ganze stuhlzusich.
Pferch.   Ueberzwerch.
(Apropos: man substrahiere Geschlechtskrankheiten;
coitus würde allgemein beliebtes Gesellschaftsspiel;
wäre im Laden zu haben. Basta.)

Best Plaster Also Red Blessing

Crockery tumbling on the ground:
just as sweet drinking Ninalla's Lips Pommery greno ridge.
Minkoff, an entire a Russian, distracts side-tracking.
Hand's palm flapping by: utilized bosom swells blond.
Lump sum.   Some.
Gulp wine (length: 63 centimeters) spit into red improved nostrils
spot.   Fat!!!
Since brave band whispers Kuno fat rump.
Knäud, whose sweaty forearm withdraws.
Thundered forward: Sibi shrieked naturally immensely,
Hemispheres overhead.
Presently burning pedal slides delighted elsewhere stroked
Belly.   Jelly.
Unrevised wipes its tongue along fattest thighs, Isidor.
Oh how I love life's riff-raff (at night, naturally!)
Kruschewaz stares at Zuzzi's oh so remote delta folds.
Baynes destiny (Massachusetts — most hospitable) flows fiddle-wantonly
                        around the corner;
Sheet-metal staggers arduously up from it:
trimmed in delicate black crepe abdomen (?Gaby!) undulates discreetly
        nearby.
"Honesty is no hollow tooth" . . . (crossing of bag and baggage)
Very skilfully Madame V. braids a glass into Roger's fingers;
crushes the whole works with seated assurance
Pen.   Again.
(In this connection: if venereal disease were eliminated;
coitus would become everyone's favorite party game;
every store would have to carry it. Enough.)

Philippe Soupault

Like the other founders of Surrealism, Philippe Soupault (1897–1973) honed his poetic skills as a member of Paris Dada. One of the cofounders of *Littérature*, with André Breton and Louis Aragon, he contributed to a great many journals and published several books of poetry. His collaboration with Breton on *Les Champs magnétiques* (1919) led to the creation of an automatic text that was to be the cornerstone of Surrealism.

Salutations distinguées

Bateaux lanternes sourdes
tout cela encore
et le cri des oiseaux
Bateaux allumettes gares
tout cela encore
tout cela
tout
Vous êtes là
moi aussi

Flamme

Une enveloppe déchirée aggrandit ma chambre
Je bouscule mes souvenirs
On part
J'avais oublié ma valise

Les Sentiments sont gratuits

Trace odeur de soufre
marais des salubrités publiques
rouge des lèvres criminelles
Marche deux temps saumure
caprice des singes
horloge couleur du jour.

Cordial Greetings

Boats muffled lanterns
all that again
and the cry of the birds
Boats matches stations
all that again
all that
all
You are there
me too

Flame

A torn envelope enlarges my room
I jostle my memories
Departure
I had forgotten my suitcase

No Charge for the Sentiments

Trace odor of sulfur
swamp of public sanitation
lipstick of criminal lips
March double time brine
caprice of monkeys
clock color of day.

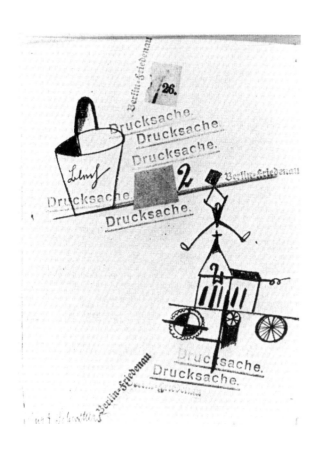

Kurt Schwitters, *Printed Matter* (© Estate of Kurt
Schwitters / VAGA, New York, 1991).

Guillermo de Torre

Guillermo de Torre (1900–72) founded the Spanish Ultraist movement together with Rafael Cansinos-Asséns. Following World War I, he was the chief conduit between Madrid and Paris and busied himself with the diffusion of Dada in Spain. His essays and poems appeared in a wide range of Spanish periodicals, including *Grecia*, *Ultra*, *Vertical*, and *Cosmópolis*, and in French publications such as *Ça Ira*, *La Vie des Lettres*, and Francis Picabia's *Le Pilhaou-Thibaou*. Torre's monumental *Literaturas europeas de vanguardia* was published in 1925.

1 4 2 2 —M

A Tristan Tzara

La matricula del automóvil rojo
red de miradas excéntricas
en la interferencia de colores
giran falenas   leticias del vértigo
lluvia de senos astrales
para los sitibundos astrólogos
ante los tranvías embarazados
los faroles saludan másculos
surgen maniquíes desnudas
las casas suben en los tranvías
las risas fluidifican el camino
todo afluye centrípeto
los motores lamen mis manos
en la yuxtaposición planista
se multiplican las diplopias
y en el vórtice nouménico
de cerebros y automóviles
una interrogación cygnea

1 4 2 2 —M

For Tristan Tzara

The red automobile's licence plate
net of eccentric glances
in the interference of colors
moths wheel   frenzied joys
rain of astral breasts
for the thirsty astrologers
before the embarrassed streetcars
the streetlights issue masculine greetings
naked mannequins suddenly appear
the houses board the streetcars
laughter liquifies the road
everything flows centripetally
the motors lick my hands
in the two-dimensional juxtaposition
double vision multiplies
and in the noumenal whirlpool
of brains and automobiles
a cygnetic question

Ruedas

ONDULACIÓN de las risas colores
en la pantalla aventura galante
la vida turbina sin corriente
y los instintos maquinistas
las palomas dan la hora
sobre la pista solar corridas
cinema de los sexos disfrazados
en el cielo de ocasión
he aquí la clave occidental
todo ama canta y vibra
los hombres atlantes
que llevan a su espalda un hemisferio
los genios de los manicomios
y tú francis picabia
a quien dedico este poema
maquinista temerario
de las locomotoras huérfanas dadaístas
yo os saludo
silbido internacional

Wheels

Colors undulation of laughter
love affair on the screen
life turbine with no current
and the instincts engineers
the doves announce the hour
bullfights on the solar rink
cinema of the disguised sexes
in the secondhand sky
here I have the western key
everything loves sings and vibrates
men Atlases
who carry a hemisphere on their shoulders
the geniuses of the mental hospitals
and you francis picabia
to whom I dedicate this poem
reckless engineer
of Dada's orphaned locomotives
I salute you
international whistling

Bric-a-brac

APOTEOSIS VIBRACIONISTA
OH EL FILM DE NUESTRAS VIDAS VERTICALES
HAY REFRACCIONES DEL ARTE NEGRO
AMBICIÓN CREATRIZ AVIÓNICA
LAS IMÁGENES TIENEN UN RITMO
        DE BALLET RUSO PLURICOLOR
LA HÉLICE DE LOS ORTOS CANTA EN LA NOCHE
FOX-TROTT LUNAR EN EL CABARET ASTRAL
Y SU SEXO   TRIÁNGULO DE AZUL
ACROBACIAS MENTALES
ALAS   MOTORES   ADIOSES
IRRADIACIÓN DE LOS INSTINTOS VIAJEROS
MADRID   PARÍS   NEW-YORK
        ZURICH   MOSCÚ
ESTACIÓN DADÁ
                TORRE EIFFEL
                        DESEMBARCADERO POLAR
CUÁNDO ES LA INAUGURACIÓN
        DEL F. C. INTERPLANETARIO?
HIPER-MUSICALES JAZZ-BAND
        RITMIZAN LAS PASIONES
                DE FÉMINAS AURÍVORAS
ADMIRAD ESE PRESTIDIGITADOR DE ESTRELLAS
LAS AVENIDAS SURCAN
        UN ARCO TRIUNFAL DE ESPEJOS
MUTACIÓN DE LOS PAISAJES ÁRTICOS
Y LOS TROLLEYS QUE ENHEBRAN AVIONES
DISPAROS EN LA PANTALLA FEÉRICA
HE AQUÍ CHARLOT PRECURSOR DADAÍSTA
LAS ESTATUAS ERRANTES
        MASTICAN CHEWING-GUM
LOS HORIZONTES SE CONTORSIONAN
DISPONED LOS PARACAÍDAS
LUMINARIAS SÁDICAS
POLIFONIZAN LOS TIMBRES
VIBRAN LAS ANTENAS
ES LA HORA POLIMORFA
Y YO ATERRIZARÉ MAÑANA

Bric-a-brac

VIBRATIONIST APOTHEOSIS
OH THE FILM OF OUR VERTICAL LIVES
THERE ARE REFRACTIONS OF NEGRO ART
AMBITION AVIONIC CREATOR
THE IMAGES HAVE A VARIEGATED
      RUSSIAN BALLET RHYTHM
THE RISING STARS' PROPELLER SINGS IN THE NIGHT
LUNAR FOX-TROT IN THE ASTRAL CABARET
AND ITS SEX   BLUE TRIANGLE
MENTAL ACROBATICS
WINGS   MOTORS   GOOD-BYES
IRRADIATION OF THE TRAVELING INSTINCTS
MADRID   PARIS   NEW YORK
     ZURICH   MOSCOW
DADA STATION
      EIFFEL TOWER
         POLAR WHARF
WHEN IS THE INAUGURATION
     OF THE INTERPLANETARY RAILROAD?
HYPERMUSICAL JAZZ BANDS
     GIVE RHYTHM TO THE PASSIONS
        OF GOLD-DIGGING FEMALES
ADMIRE THIS CONJURER OF STARS
THE AVENUES PLOW AHEAD
     A TRIUMPHAL ARCH OF MIRRORS
MUTATION OF THE ARCTIC REGIONS
AND THE STREETCARS THAT STRING AIRPLANES TOGETHER
SHOTS ON THE MAGIC SCREEN
HERE IS CHARLIE CHAPLIN A DADA PRECURSOR
THE WANDERING STATUES
     CHEW CHEWING GUM
THE HORIZONS CONTORT THEMSELVES
PREPARE THE SAFETY NETS
SADISTIC LANTERNS
POLYPHONIZE THE BELLS
VIBRATE THE ANTENNAS
IT IS THE POLYMORPHOUS HOUR
AND I WILL LAND TOMORROW

Tristan Tzara

Tristan Tzara (1896–1963) was the unofficial head of the international Dada movement. Born in Romania, he came to Zurich during World War I and cofounded the Dada group there. The author of countless manifestos, numerous poems, and several important plays, he contributed to nearly all the Dada journals that were published. As the editor of *Dada* and later as the coeditor of *Der Zeltweg*, Tzara corresponded with Dada factions all over the world and provided the most important unifying force. In 1920 he arrived in Paris where he edited *Le Coeur à Barbe* and continued his Dada activities.

Le Marin

il fait l'amour avec une femme qui n'a qu'une jambe
l'étroitesse d'un anneau pondichéry
on a ouvert son ventre qui grince grigri

d'où sortent les bas et les animaux oblongs
dans ton intérieur il y a des lampes fumantes
le marais de miel bleu
chat accroupi dans l'or d'une taverne flamande
boum boum
beaucoup de sable bicycliste jaune
château neuf des papes
manhattan il y a des baquets d'excrément devant toi
mbaze mbaze bazebaze mleganga garoo
tu circules rapidement en moi
kangourous dans les entrailles du bateau
attends je vais premièrement arranger mes impressions
les excursionnistes assis dentelle au bord de l'eau
enfonce les doigts dans les orbites que la lumière crève grenades
l'urubu nous regarde — tu dois rentrer dans la ménagerie des
    intelligences
l'urubu s'enracine dans le ciel en ulcère orange
où vas-tu
prestidigitateur moulin à vent coiffures tous les pygargues sont
    chancreux
egg-nogg

The Sailor

He is making love to a woman who has only one leg
the tightness of a Pondichery ring
they have opened his stomach which shrieks chi-chi

from which come the stockings and the oblong animals
in your interior there are smoking lamps
the blue honey swamp
cat crouching in the gold of a Flemish tavern
boom boom
lots of sand yellow cyclist
new chateau for the popes
Manhattan there are tubs of excrement before you
mbaze mbaze bazebaze mleganga garoo
you circulate rapidly in me
kangaroos in the ship's entrails
wait I will first arrange my impressions
the seated travelers lace on the water's edge
stick your fingers in the orbits that the light punctures pomegranates
the tropical vulture watches us—you must reenter the menagerie
            of understanding
the tropical vulture takes root in the sky as an orange ulcer
where are you going
conjurer windmill hair styles all the ospreys are cankerous
egg-nog

La Panka

De la teeee ee erre moooooonte
    des bouuuules
Là aaa aaaaaa oû oùoù pououou
    oussent les clarinettes
De l'intééé eee eee eee rieur mo onte
    des boules vers la suuu uurfa
    aaa aace
Negrigrigrigriiiillons dans les nuuuuu a aaages
je déchiiiiiiire la colliiiiiiiiiii
ine le tapiiii ii iii iii is je fais
un graaaaaaaaaand panaaaaaaankaa
neee ma teeechnintes et yayayaya
tagaaa a aaan insomnie inie
iaoai xixixi xixi cla cla clo
drrrrrrrrrrrrrrrrrrrrrrrrrrrrr

Sage Danse deux

accroissement d'un brouillard d'hélices imprévues
arc voltaïque impassible visse
les corridors   échine des maisons et la fumée
gradation du vent qui déchire le linge
dans un tiroir la tabatière écorces d'oranges et des ficelles
o soupape de mon âme vidée
la fiole liée au cou
les trains se taisent tout d'un coup

The Punka

From the eaaaa aa arth spheeeeeeres
 asceeeeend
There rre rrrre where wherewhere the clararar
 arinettes sprout
From the inteee eee eee eee rior sphe eres
 ascend toward the suuu uurfa
 aaa aace
Blackchichichichiiiildren in the clooooo u uuuds
I teaaaaaar the hiiiiiiiiiii
ill the carpeeee ee eee eee et I make
a greaaaaaaaaaat punuuuuuunkaa
neee my teeechnintes and yayayaya
tagaaa a aaan insomnia inia
iaoai xixixi xixi cla cla clo
drrrrrrrrrrrrrrrrrrrrrrrrrrrrrrr

Wise Dance Two

growth of a fog of unforeseen propellers
electric arc impassive screws
the corridors the houses' spine and the smoke
the wind's gradation which tears the linen
in a drawer the humidor orange peels and strings
oh safety valve of my emptied soul
the vial tied to one's neck
suddenly the trains fall silent

Printemps

A Hans Arp

placer l'enfant dans le vase au fond de minuit
et la plaie
une rose des vents avec tes doigts aux beaux ongles
le tonnerre dans des plumes voir
une eau mauvaise coule des membres de l'antilope

souffrir en bas avez-vous trouvé des vaches des oiseaux?
la soif le fiel du paon dans la cage
le roi en exil par la clarté du puits se momifie lentement
dans le jardin de légumes
semer des sauterelles brisées
planter des coeurs de fourmis le brouillard de sel une lampe tire la
        queue sur le ciel
les petits éclats de verreries   dans le ventre des cerfs en fuite
sur les points des branches noires courtes   pour un cri

Spring

For Hans Arp

to place the child in the vase in the depths of midnight
and the wound
a compass-card with your fingers and beautiful nails
the thunder in feathers to see
a foul liquid flows from the antelope's limbs

to suffer below have you found some cows some birds?
thirst the spleen of the peacock in the cage
the king in exile by the clarity of the well slowly mummifies
in the vegetable garden
to sow some broken grasshoppers
to plant some hearts of ants the salt fog a lamp pulls the tail
    on the sky
the shards of glass   in the bellies of the fleeing deer
on the points of the short black branches   for a cry

Hendrik Nicolaas Werkman

Not a great deal is known about Hendrik Nicolaas Werkman (1882–1945), whose typographical compositions link him to the Constructivists and to Holland Dada. The owner of a printing business in Groningen, he edited a journal with an English title, *The Next Call*, from 1923 to 1926. His interest in geometric art, architecture, and design reflects that of the De Stijl group and of individuals such as Theo van Doesburg and Til Brugman. Like them, he was a precursor of the Concrete poetry movement.

VANITE

HOTEL

du 1er ordre

Reaction

reaction

ZiE oP u zeLf

140 ton

jemaintiendrai Maandag

Maandag

**breedsprakigheid
in alle talen**

BELEEFDHEID

DEUGD

DIKKE TONG

rang

&

stand

HOUDING

VANITY
1st class
HOTEL
Reaction
reaction
Look at yourself
140 Ton

Twillstandfast Monday
Monday
verbosity
in all languages
POLITENESS
VIRTUE
FAT TONGUE
rank
&
station
BEARING

Selected Bibliography

Selected Bibliography

Ades, Dawn. *Dada and Surrealism*. Woodbury, N.Y.: Barron's, 1978.

————. *Dada and Surrealism Reviewed*. London: Arts Council of Great Britain, 1978.

Bigsby, Christopher W. E. *Dada and Surrealism*. London: Methuen, 1972.

Caws, Mary Ann. *The Poetry of Dada and Surrealism*. Princeton, N.J.: Princeton University Press, 1970.

Coutts-Smith, Kenneth. *Dada*. New York: Dutton, 1970.

Dada/Surrealism. Edited by Rudolf E. Kuenzli and Mary Ann Caws. No. 1 (1971)–.

Foster, Stephen C. *Dada Dimensions*. Ann Arbor: UMI Research Press, 1985.

Foster, Stephen C., and Rudolf E. Kuenzli. *Dada Spectrum: The Dialectics of Revolt*. Madison: Coda, Iowa City: University of Iowa, 1979.

Foster, Stephen C., Rudolf E. Kuenzli, and Richard Sheppard. *Dada Artifacts*. Iowa City: University of Iowa Museum of Art, 1978.

Grossman, Manuel L. *Dada: Paradox, Mystification, and Ambiguity in European Literature*. New York: Bobbs-Merrill, 1971.

Lippard, Lucy R. *Dadas on Art*. Englewood Cliffs, N.J.: Prentice-Hall, 1971.

Matthews, J. H. *Theatre in Dada and Surrealism*. Syracuse, N.Y.: Syracuse University Press, 1974.

Motherwell, Robert. *The Dada Painters and Poets: An Anthology*. 2d ed. Cambridge, Mass.: Belknap, 1989.

Richter, Hans. *Dada: Art and Anti-Art*. Translated by David Britt. London: Thames and Hudson, 1965.

Rubin, William S. *Dada, Surrealism, and Their Heritage*. New York: Museum of Modern Art, 1968.

Russell, Charles. *Poets, Prophets, and Revolutionaries: The Literary Avant-Garde from Rimbaud through Postmodernism*. Oxford: Oxford University Press, 1985.

Tashjian, Dickran. *Skyscraper Primitives: Dada and the American Avant-*

Garde, 1910–1925. Middletown, Conn.: Wesleyan University Press, 1975.

Verkauf, Willy. *Dada: Monograph of a Movement*. London: Academy, New York: St. Martin's, 1975.

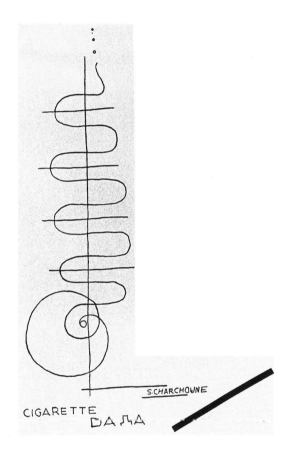

Serge Charchoune, *Dada Cigarette* (COPYRIGHT
1992 ARS, N.Y. / ADAGP).

Willard Bohn received his doctorate from the University of California at Berkeley where he was a Chancellor's Fellow. He has taught at Brandeis University, the University of California at Santa Cruz, and Illinois State University. He is presently professor of foreign languages at the latter institution and was recently designated as Outstanding University Researcher. He is the author of more than sixty articles and four books devoted to avant-garde subjects, including *Apollinaire and the Faceless Man*; *The Aesthetics of Visual Poetry*; *Apollinaire, Visual Poetry, and Art Criticism*; and *Apollinaire and the International Avant-Garde*. He has been the recipient of grants or fellowships from the National Endowment for the Humanities, the American Council of Learned Societies, the American Philosophical Society, the Fulbright-Hays Commission, the Camargo Foundation, and the Institut Français de Washington.